Revision Notes
for
Standard Grade
Physics

D1324798

Lyn Robinson

Principal Teacher of Physics

Williamwood High School, Clarkston

Editorial work assisted by Jim Jardine
and
Campbell White
(Principal Teacher of Physics,
Tynecastle High School)

Published by
Chemcord
Inch Keith
East Kilbride
Glasgow

ISBN   1 870570 51 0

© Robinson, 1993

First reprint 1995
Second reprint 1997
Third reprint 1999
Fourth Reprint 2003

Printed by Bell and Bain Ltd, Glasgow

Note to student

● **The course**

This book is designed to cover all of the learning outcomes of the Standard Grade Physics syllabus for examinations in 1994 onwards.

Exam structure

● General Paper $1\,^1/_2$ hours   approximately 90 marks, close to an equal split between Knowledge and Understanding and Problem Solving

● Credit Paper $1\,^3/_4$ hours   approximately 100 marks, close to an equal split between Knowledge and Understanding and Problem Solving

● Practical Abilities are assessed within the school.

Symbols in the book

● ❏   General level material   ○   Credit level material

Using the book

● You can indicate your knowledge of each statement with a tick in the box at the left hand side.

● Space has been left at the right hand side so that you can make additional notes.

● You can also mark statements with a highlighter pen.

Exam advice

● Make sure that you have a calculator, ruler, pen, pencil and rubber.

● Draw a graph lightly in pencil; when you are certain it is correct, go over in ink.

● In numerical questions always put the information into symbol form and check it is in basic units.

● Remember to give units for all answers.

● Working through past papers is an essential part of your preparation.

Revision checklist

		Tick (√) when revised			
		1	**2**	**3**	**4**
Telecommunications	1. Communication using waves				
	2. Waves				
	3. Radio and television				
	4. Optical fibres				
	5. Satellites and dish aerials				
Using Electricity	1. From the wall socket				
	2. Alternating and direct current				
	3. Resistance				
	4. Useful circuits				
	5. Behind the wall				
	6. Movement from electricty				
Health Physics	1. The use thermometers				
	2. Using sound				
	3. Light and sound				
	4. Using the spectrum				
	5. Nuclear radiation - humans and medicine				
Electronics	1. Overview				
	2. Output devices				
	3. Input devices				
	4. Digital processes				
	5. Analogue processes				
Transport	1. On the move				
	2. Forces at work				
	3. Movement means energy				
Energy Matters	1. Supply and demand				
	2. Generation of electricity				
	3. Source to consumer				
	4. Heat in the home				
Space Physics	1. Signals from space				
	2. Space travel				

UNIT 1 TELECOMMUNICATIONS

Section 1 Communicating using waves

- ❑ The speed of sound in air is less than the speed of light in air.

- ❑ The speed of sound in air is about 330 m s^{-1};
  the speed of light in air is 3×10^{8} m s^{-1}.

- ❑ An example which shows this difference is thunder and lightning; the thunder is heard after the lightning is seen, although both are produced at the same time.

- ❑ **Speed** has the symbol ***v***, and is measured in metres per second, **m s^-1^**.

- ❑ **Distance** has the symbol ***d***, and is measured in metres, **m**.

- ❑ **Time** has the symbol ***t***, and is measured in seconds, **s**.

- ❑ These quantities are related by the equation:

$$d = v t$$

- ❑ *Example*
  How far will sound travel in 1 minute?

Step 1 Put the information into symbol form and change to basic units.

v = 330 m s^{-1}
t = 1 minute = 60 s

Step 2 Choose the correct equation.

$d = v t$

Step 3 Put the numbers into the equation and calculate the answer.

$d = v t$ = 330 x 60 = **19 800 m**

DO NOT FORGET UNITS.

Measuring the speed of sound in air

❑ Large cymbals are clashed a long distance, **d**, from an observer; a stopwatch is started when the cymbals are seen to move and stopped when the sound is heard; the time, **t**, for the sound to travel the distance, **d**, is noted; the equation $v = \dfrac{d}{t}$

can be used to calculate the speed of sound; for accuracy, the process is repeated and the average taken.

❑ A second method uses a computer:

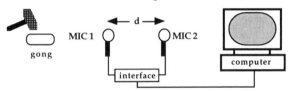

When the gong is hit, sound travels to the microphone, MIC 1, and starts the computer clock; when the sound reaches MIC 2 the clock is stopped and the time, **t**, registered on the computer; this is the time for the sound to travel a distance, **d**; the equation $v = \dfrac{d}{t}$

can be used to calculate the speed of sound.

A Morse Code transmitter

❑

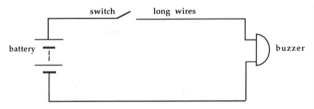

❑ When the switch is held down the buzzer sounds; holding down for a long time gives a dash and for a short time gives a dot; the Morse Code uses combinations of dots and dashes to represent letters and numbers.

❑ A **transmitter** sends out a signal.

❑ A **receiver** collects and replays the signal.

❏ Advantages of sending messages through wires rather than through the air include:

(1) messages can usually be kept private,
(2) messages can be sent over long distances,
(3) messages can be sent very fast,
(4) simple transmitting and receiving equipment.

❏ Using the telephone is an example of sending messages through wires.

❏ The transmitter in the telephone is the mouthpiece; the mouthpiece contains a microphone.

❏ The receiver in the telephone is the earpiece; the earpiece contains an earphone, ie. a small loudspeaker.

❏ The energy changes are:
microphone: sound ⟶ electrical

loudspeaker: electrical ⟶ sound

❏ Telephone signals travel along the wires as electrical signals; they travel along the wires at about 2.9×10^8 m s^{-1}, ie. approaching the speed of light which is 3×10^8 m s^{-1}.

❏ The signal pattern in the telephone wires can be seen on an oscilloscope.

❏ When the sound signal gets louder, the amplitude increases:

quiet   **loud**

❏ When the frequency of the signal increases, the pitch of the note is higher:

low frequency   **high frequency**

○   The electric signal in telephone wires undergoes the same changes as the sound signal, ie. as the sound gets louder the electric signal has a larger amplitude;
as the pitch of the sound gets higher, the frequency of the electric signal increases.

❑   If two notes are an **octave** apart (eight notes apart on the musical scale) the frequency of one is double the other,
eg. middle C, f = 262 Hz
      high C, f = 524 Hz

Section 2   Waves

❑   Waves carry energy from place to place;
     therefore waves can carry signals from place to place.

❑   The **amplitude** is the height of the wave measured from
     the centre to the top of a crest **or** to the bottom of a
     trough;
     it has the symbol **a**, and is measured in metres, **m**.

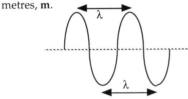

❑   The **wavelength** is the distance from one point on a crest
     or trough to the same point on the next one;
     it has the symbol λ, (lambda), and is measured in

     metres, **m**.

❑   The amplitude is a measure of the energy carried by a
     wave; the larger the amplitude, the more energy is being
     carried by the wave and thus the stronger the signal.

❑   The **frequency** is the number of waves per second;
     it has the symbol **f**, and is measured in hertz, **Hz**.

❑   The **period** is the time taken for one wave to pass;
     it has the symbol **T**, and is measured in seconds, **s**.

❑ $$T = \frac{1}{f}$$ or $$f = \frac{1}{T}$$

❑   The wave equation is:

     $$v = f\,\lambda$$ where **v** is the speed in m s^{-1}
                                  f is the frequency in Hz
                                  λ is the wavelength in m

○ The two expressions for wave speed

$$v = f\,\lambda \quad \text{and} \quad v = \frac{d}{t}$$

can be shown to be equivalent:

Waves move one wavelength in a time equal to one period.

Thus when $d = \lambda$ then $t = T = \dfrac{1}{f}$

Therefore $v = \dfrac{d}{T} = \dfrac{\lambda}{\frac{1}{f}} = f\,\lambda$

Choose the most suitable equation for the information given.

❑ **Example**
A wave travels 50 cm in 5 s.
If its frequency is 2 Hz, find
(a) its speed,
(b) its wavelength.

Step 1 Put the information into symbol form and change to basic units.

$d = 50\,\text{cm} = 0.5\,\text{m}$
$t = 5\,\text{s}$
$f = 2\,\text{Hz}$

Step 2 Choose the correct equation for part (a).

$$d = v\,t \;\Rightarrow\; v = \frac{d}{t}$$

Step 3 Put the numbers into the equation and calculate the answer.

$$v = \frac{d}{t} = \frac{0.5}{5} = 0.1\,\text{m s}^{-1}$$

Repeat steps 2 and 3 for part (b).

$$v = f\,\lambda \;\Rightarrow\; \lambda = \frac{v}{f} = \frac{0.1}{2} = 0.05\,\text{m}$$

DO NOT FORGET UNITS.

Section 3   Radio and television

❑   Radio and television are examples of long range communication which do not need wires between the transmitter and the receiver.

❑   Radio and television signals are carried by waves which transfer energy.

❑   Radio and television signals are transmitted at a very high speed through the air, 300 000 000 m s⁻¹.

○   Use $v = 3 \times 10^8$ m s⁻¹ with the equation $d = v\,t$ to find the distance travelled or the time taken by radio and television signals.

Parts of a radio receiver

❑   AERIAL   collects all the signals of various frequencies and converts them to small electric currents

❑   TUNER   selects one particular carrier frequency

❑   DECODER   changes the a.c. signal into a d.c. signal

         a.c.   d.c.

❑   AMPLIFIER   makes the signal larger so that it can drive the loudspeaker

❑   LOUDSPEAKER   changes electrical energy into sound energy

❑   ELECTRICITY SUPPLY   provides energy for the amplifier

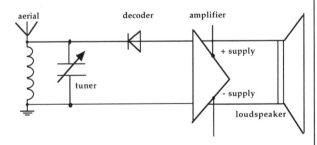

○ To transmit sound by radio a high frequency carrier wave is added to the sound (audio) signal at the transmitter;
this can make the amplitude of the carrier wave change, ie. the wave has the same frequency but a varying amplitude;
this is called **amplitude modulation (AM)**:

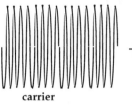 + =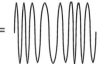

carrier	**audio**	**amplitude**
wave	**signal**	**modulated (AM)**
		wave

○ The carrier wave can keep the same amplitude and carry the audio signal by changing its frequency; this is called **frequency modulation (FM)**, ie. the wave has the same amplitude but a varying frequency:

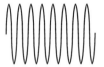 + =

carrier	**audio**	**frequency**
wave	**signal**	**modulated**
		(FM) wave

○ Frequency modulation produces higher quality signals.

○ The sound signal is restored by removing the carrier wave from the modulated signal at the receiver (demodulation); this is done by the decoder.

❏ Each radio transmitter has its own particular frequency and wavelength,
eg. Radio Scotland 810 kHz/ 370 m.

○ Use $v = 3 \times 10^8$ m s^{-1} with the equation $v = f\lambda$ to find the frequency or the wavelength of radio waves.

○ **Diffraction** is the bending of waves round corners; long wavelength waves diffract more than short wavelengths:

○

long wavelength   **short wavelength**

○ Since radio waves have longer wavelengths than television waves, reception for radio is better than for television when the receiver is behind hills.

○ **Properties of radio bands**

ELF (extra low frequency) - pass through water;
30 - 3000 Hz   used with submarines

LF (low frequency)   - reflect off ionosphere;
3 - 300 kHz   travel long distances
(long waves)

HF (high frequency)   - travel close to ground; used
0.3 - 30 MHz   for local radio (medium);
(medium or short wave)   short waves have world
                                             wide range by reflections
                                             from the ionosphere

VHF (very high   - travel in straight lines into
frequency)   space; used for FM;
30 - 300 MHz   short range due to
                                             curvature of Earth's surface

UHF (ultra high   - used for television
frequency)
300 - 3000 MHz

Microwaves   - pass through ionosphere;
> 3000 MHz   used for satellite
                                             communication

❏ **Parts of a television receiver**

```
                 ┌──────────┐   ┌──────────┐   ┌─────────┐
                 │ Vision   │───│ Vision   │───│ Picture │
                 │ decoder  │   │ amplifier│   │ tube    │
            ▲    └──────────┘   └──────────┘   └─────────┘
┌──────┐ ┌─────┐
│Aerial├─┤Tuner│
└──────┘ └─────┘
            ▼    ┌──────────┐   ┌──────────┐   ┌─────────────┐
                 │ Audio    │───│ Audio    │   │ Loudspeaker │
                 │ decoder  │   │ amplifier│   │             │
                 └──────────┘   └──────────┘   └─────────────┘
```

❏ These parts have the same function in the TV as the corresponding parts of a radio; the energy change in the picture tube is from electrical to light energy.

❏ The energy for the amplifiers comes from the electricity supply.

○ The television signal is sent in the same way as the radio signal except that there are two signals, one audio and one visual, which have to be synchronised (occur at the same time).

❏ There are 625 lines on the television screen, these combine to form the picture.

○ Each line is formed by an electron beam hitting the screen and moving across the screen; when the beam hits the phosphors on the screen the kinetic energy of the electrons changes into light energy.

○ The production of these 625 lines is called **scanning.**

○ A new picture is produced 25 times per second and because our eyes retain the image on the retina for 1/20th of a second, we do not see separate pictures; each merges into the last.

○ Movement is produced by making each picture slightly different from the last.

❏ Brightness is varied by changing the number of electrons hitting any part of the screen.

Colour mixing

❏ The three **primary** colours are: red
                                                  blue
                                                  green

○ The three **secondary** colours are: yellow
                                                  cyan (turquoise)
                                                  magenta

○ Each is produced by two primary colours:

red	+	blue	=	magenta
red	+	green	=	yellow
green	+	blue	=	cyan

❏ The colour television screen has sets of three primary coloured dots at each point on the screen; one electron gun fires at each coloured dot and by varying the numbers of electrons hitting each colour they are lit up with varying intensities; this allows all colours to be produced by colour mixing.

Section 4   Optical fibres

❑   An optical fibre is a thin clear thread of glass, along which light can travel.

❑   Optical fibres and electrical cables are used to carry telephone messages;
the signal travels at about 2×10^8 m s^{-1}.

○   Advantages of optical fibres over electrical cables are:

(1)   cheaper to make,
(2)   much smaller in size,
(3)   can carry a larger number of signals,
(4)   no electrical interference,
(5)   cannot easily be 'tapped',
(6)   less energy lost, so fewer repeater stations needed.

Properties of light

○   Light travels in straight lines and ray paths are reversible.

❑   **Reflection**
Light can be reflected.

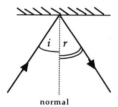

i = angle of incidence
r = angle of reflection

The law of reflection states that the angle of incidence is equal to the angle of reflection.

○   **Refraction**
Light is usually bent when it travels from one material into another because the light travels more slowly in the material than the air.
The angle to the normal is always largest in air.

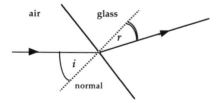

○ When light travels from glass to air, it bends away from the normal; as the angle of incidence is increased the last ray of light which can escape meets the boundary at the **critical angle** (C) and emerges at 90° to the normal:

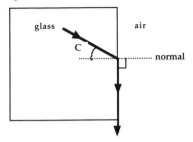

○ Any ray incident on the boundary at an angle greater than the critical angle will undergo **total internal reflection (TIR)**.

○ Light travels along optical fibres by total internal reflection:

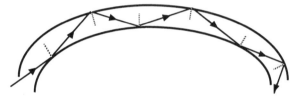

❑ The signal is made up of variations in the light and these are transmitted very quickly to the other end of the optical fibre.

○ Use $v = 2 \times 10^8$ m s^{-1} for the speed of light in an optical fibre and the equation $d = v\,t$ to find the distance travelled or the time taken.

Section 5   Satellites and dish aerials

❑   The **period** of a satellite (time taken for it to orbit the Earth) depends on the height above the Earth.

❑   A **geostationary satellite** orbits in 24 hours and therefore stays above the same point on the Earth's surface.

❑   Three geostationary satellites on the equator allow world-wide communication, with each satellite linking with ground stations on different continents.

○   A **ground station** uses a curved reflector to transmit the microwave signal as a parallel beam to the satellite:

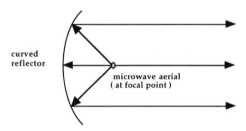

❑   The satellite has a curved reflector to collect the signal over a large area and bring it to a **focus**; the receiver aerial is placed at the focus.

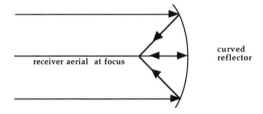

❑   At the satellite the signal is amplified and its frequency changed it is then sent back to Earth; this time the transmitter sends out a signal and the curved reflector ensures a parallel beam and the curved satellite dish on houses, etc. collects the signal over the large area of the dish and focuses it to make the signal stronger.

UNIT 2   USING ELECTRICITY

Section 1   From the wall socket

❑   The mains supplies electrical energy.

❑   The energy transformations (changes) for some
    household appliances are:

electric fire	- electricity to heat (and light)
cooker	- electricity to heat
vacuum cleaner	- electricity to movement (and sound and heat)
kettle	- electricity to heat
hairdryer	- electricity to movement and heat
light bulb	- electricity to light (and heat)
television	- electricity to light and sound

❑   Typical power ratings are:

electric fire	-	3000 W
cooker	-	12 000 W
vacuum cleaner	-	600 W
kettle	-	2000 W
hairdryer	-	1000 W
light bulb	-	60 - 100 W
television	-	250 W

❑   The correct flex must be used with each appliance;
    the flex must be thick enough to carry the current
    without overheating; an appliance with a higher
    power rating needs a thicker flex.

❑   The **fuse** is in the plug to cut off the mains supply if
    there is a risk of overheating; this protects the flex
    (and the appliance) from damage.

❑   In general, the correct fuse for an electrical appliance
    is:

    3 A for an appliance up to 675 W
    13 A for an appliance of more than 675 W

❑   The colour code for plug wiring is:

live	-	brown
neutral	-	blue
earth	-	green and yellow

❑   The live wire in a plug is always connected to the
    fuse; the earth wire is connected to the top pin.

❑   The human body conducts electricity.

❑   Water makes the human body a better conductor.

❑   The earth wire is a safety device.

○   The earth wire is connected to the metal casing of the appliance; if a fault develops and the live wire touches the casing, there is a path to earth and the appliance remains safe.

○   The live wire is connected to the high dangerous voltage, while the neutral wire is at zero or earth voltage; both the switch and the fuse are connected to the live wire so that they can cut off the high voltage and leave the appliance safe.

❑   Appliances which are entirely cased in plastic are **double insulated** and do not need the earth wire.

❑   The double insulation symbol is:

❑   3 core flex is used for most appliances;
     2 core flex is used for double insulated appliances.

❑   **Dangerous situations** include:

     (1) using electricity near water;
          this makes shocks more dangerous,
     (2) wrong fuses;
          this can allow overheating to take place,
     (3) wrongly connected flexes;
          this can leave the appliance live even when switched off,
     (4) frayed, or badly connected, flex;
          this can give a shock,
     (5) too many appliances on the same socket or using multiway adaptors;
          this can draw too much current from the mains and therefore cause overheating.

Section 2   Alternating and direct current

❑   **Direct current** (d.c.) is always in the same direction; electrons flow from negative to positive.

❑   **Alternating current** (a.c.) changes direction many times every second.

❑   The mains supply is a.c.

❑   A battery supply is d.c.

❑   An oscilloscope can show these patterns:

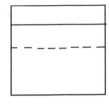 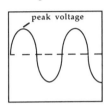

        d.c.   **a.c.**

❑   The frequency of the mains supply is 50 Hz.

❑   The mains voltage is 230 V.

○   The quoted voltage of an a.c. supply, eg. 230 V for the mains, is the average (root mean square - r.m.s.) value and is less than the peak value (325 V for the mains).

❑   An electric current is caused by the movement of charges (negative electrons) round a circuit.

❑   A **conductor** allows electric current to pass through it because electrons are free to move.

❑   **Current** has the symbol *I*, and is measured in amperes (amps), **A**.

❑   **Voltage** has the symbol *V*, and is measured in volts, **V**.

Circuit symbols

- ❑ cell
- ❑ battery
- ❑ fuse
- ❑ lamp
- ❑ resistor
- ❑ variable resistor
- ❑ capacitor
- ❑ diode

- ○ **Charge** has the symbol **Q**, and is measured in coulombs, **C**.

- ○ The voltage of a supply is a measure of the energy given to the charges in a circuit,
  eg. a 1.5 V battery gives 1.5 J of energy to each coulomb of charge passing through it.

- ○ Charge, current and time are related by the equation:

$$Q = I\,t$$

where **Q** is the charge in C
I is the current in A
t is the time in s

○ *Example*
What is the current when 600 C of charge is
transferred in 5 minutes?

Step 1 Put the information into symbol form and
change to basic units.

Q = 600 C
t = 5 mins = 5 x 60 = 300 s

Step 2 Choose the correct equation.

$$Q = It => \quad I = \frac{Q}{t}$$

Step 3 Put the numbers into the equation and
calculate the answer.

$$I = \frac{Q}{t} = \frac{600}{300} = 2\ A$$

DO NOT FORGET UNITS.

Section 3　Resistance

❑ Current is measured by an **ammeter**; voltage is measured by a **voltmeter**.

❑ The circuit symbols for an ammeter and a voltmeter are:

❑ An ammeter is always placed in series in the circuit.

❑ A voltmeter is always placed in parallel.

❑ **Circuit diagram**

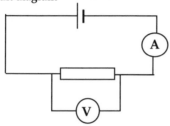

❑ Resistance has to do with the difficulty charges have in moving; it has the symbol **R**, and is measured in ohms, Ω.

❑ When the resistance in the circuit increases, the current in the circuit decreases.

○ For a given resistor, $\dfrac{V}{I}$ is approximately constant even when the current changes;

$\dfrac{V}{I}$ is called the resistance of the resistor.

❑ **Ohm's law**

$$V = IR$$

where **V** is the voltage in V
I is the current in A
R is the resistance in Ω

❑ *Example*
What current can a 240 V supply produce in a
1 kilohm resistor?

Step 1 Put the information into symbol form and
change to basic units.

V = 240 V
R = 1 kΩ = 1000 Ω

Step 2 Choose the correct equation.

$V = IR$ => $I = \dfrac{V}{R}$

Step 3 Put the numbers into the equation and
calculate the answer.

$I = \dfrac{V}{R} = \dfrac{240}{1000} = 0.24$ A

DO NOT FORGET UNITS.

❑ **Variable resistors** can alter the current;
they are used:
      as volume controls in radios, etc.
      in petrol gauges
      in strain gauges

❑ When there is an electric current in a wire, electrical
energy changes into another form of energy.

❑ Electrical energy is changed to heat in:
      an electric fire
      an electric cooker
      an electric kettle

❑ In an electric fire (heater) the energy change takes
place in the resistance wire;
this is called the **element**

❑ In a lamp, electrical energy is changed into light and
heat.

❑ There are two main types of lamp:

(1) **A filament lamp**
The energy change takes place in the filament
(resistance wire).
(2) **A discharge or fluorescent tube**
The energy change takes place in the gas.

❑ A discharge tube is more efficient than a filament lamp; more of the electrical energy is changed into light and less into heat.

❑ **Energy** has the symbol **E**, and is measured in joules, **J**.

❑ **Power** is the rate at which energy is converted into other energies;
it has the symbol **P**, and is measured in watts, **W**;
one watt is one joule per second:

$$1\,W = 1\,J\,s^{-1}$$

❑ Energy is related to power and time by the equation:

$$\boxed{E = Pt}$$ where t is the time in s

❑ *Example*
How long does it take for a 2.5 kW fire to use 30 MJ of energy?

Step 1 Put the information into symbol form and change to basic units.

P = 2.5 kW = 2500 W
E = 30 MJ = 30 000 000 J

Step 2 Choose the correct equation.

$$E = Pt \quad \Rightarrow \quad t = \frac{E}{P}$$

Step 3 Put the numbers into the equation and calculate the answer.

$$t = \frac{E}{P} = \frac{30\,000\,000}{2500} = 12\,000\,s = \textbf{200 mins}$$

DO NOT FORGET UNITS.

❑ Electrical power is related to current and voltage by the equation:

$$P = I\,V$$

where **P** is the power in W
I is the current in A
V is the voltage in V

❑ *Example*
Find the current through a 2 kW heater connected to the mains supply.

Step 1 Put the information into symbol form and change to basic units.

P = 2 kW = 2000 W
V = 230 V (mains supply)

Step 2 Choose the correct equation.

$$P = I\,V \quad \Rightarrow \quad I = \frac{P}{V}$$

Step 3 Put the numbers into the equation and calculate the answer.

$$I = \frac{P}{V} = \frac{2000}{230} = 8.7\ A$$

DO NOT FORGET UNITS.

○ Another expression for electrical power is:

$$P = I^2 R$$

where P is the power in W
I is the current in A
R is the resistance in Ω

○ *Example*
What is the power dissipated in a 10 Ω
resistor with 50 mA through it?

Step 1 Put the information into symbol form and
change to basic units.

$R = 10\,\Omega$
$I = 50\,\text{mA} = 0.05\,\text{A}$

Step 2 Choose the correct equation.

$P = I^2 R$

Step 3 Put the numbers into the equation and
calculate the answer.

$P = I^2 R = (0.05)^2 \times 10$

$= \textbf{0.025 W or 25 mW}$

DO NOT FORGET UNITS.

○ The two expressions

$P = I^2 R$ and $P = I\,V$

can be shown to be equivalent:

$P = I\,V$ but from Ohm's law $V = I\,R$

Therefore $P = I\,(I\,R)$
$\qquad\quad = I^2 R$

Section 4   Useful circuits

❏   There is only one path round a **series circuit**:

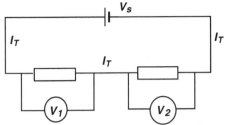

❏   The current is the same at all points in the series circuit.

❏   The supply voltage is equal to the sum of the voltages across the various components in a series circuit:

$$V_S = V_1 + V_2$$

❏   There is more than one path round a **parallel circuit**; the various paths are known as branches:

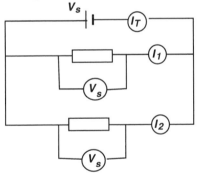

❏   The voltage across components in parallel is the same for each component .

❏   The sum of the currents in parallel branches is equal to the current drawn from the supply:

$$I_T = I_1 + I_2$$

❑ In the house, two switches are used in series when a switched appliance is plugged into a switched socket.

❑ It is dangerous to connect too many appliances to one socket because it could draw a large current (total of currents for each appliance) from the supply.

❑ A simple **continuity tester** can be made using a battery and a bulb; this can be used for fault finding.

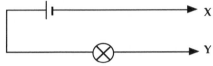

The object to be tested is placed between **X** and **Y**; if the bulb lights there is a continuous circuit and the object is a conductor.

❑ An **ohmmeter** can also check circuits:

❑ The ohmmeter will read nearly zero ohms if there is a short circuit and as high as the meter will allow if there is an open circuit (a gap in the circuit).

○ To find the total resistance R_T of resistors R_1 and R_2 connected in series the following equation is used:

$$R_T = R_1 + R_2$$

○ To find the total resistance R_T of resistors R_1 and R_2 connected in parallel the following equation is used:

$$\frac{1}{R_T} = \frac{1}{R_1} + \frac{1}{R_2}$$

○ If two identical resistors R are in parallel then R_T is $R/2$;

if three identical resistors R are in parallel then R_T is $R/3$.

○   *Example*

Find the total resistance of the following circuit.

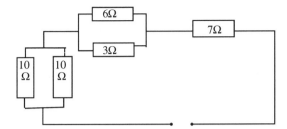

Step 1
Replace the pairs of resistors in parallel, with the single equivalent resistor.

For the two 10 Ω resistors in parallel,
$$R_T = \frac{R}{2} = 5\,\Omega$$

For the 6 Ω and the 3 Ω resistors in parallel:
$$\frac{1}{R_T} = \frac{1}{R_1} + \frac{1}{R_2} = \frac{1}{6} + \frac{1}{3}$$

Put both over a common denominator.
$$\frac{1}{R_T} = \frac{1+2}{6} = \frac{3}{6}$$

Turn both sides the other way up.
$$\frac{R_T}{1} = \frac{6}{3} = 2\,\Omega$$

Step 2

The circuit now becomes:

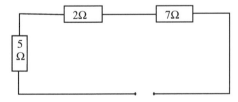

Apply resistors in series formula:
$$R_T = R_1 + R_2 + R_3$$
$$= 5 + 2 + 7 = 14\,\Omega$$

○ **Car lights,** eg. headlights and sidelights

All bulbs are placed in parallel with the battery so that each has 12 V across it:

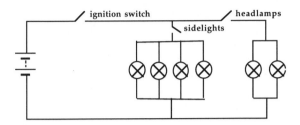

○ **Courtesy light**

This has to come on when either front door is opened; two switches in parallel are used, one for each door:

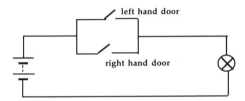

Section 5　Behind the wall

❑　All the wiring in the house connects appliances in parallel.

❑　Lighting circuits are connected in simple parallel circuits.

○　Sockets are connected in parallel by a **ring main**:

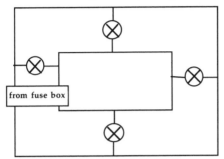

○　The ring circuit is preferred because:

(1)　the current in each wire can be halved since the current can reach the appliance from two directions, and so less energy is wasted,

(2)　thinner cable can be used with a smaller current,

(3)　there is less risk of overheating with smaller current.

○　Differences between the lighting circuit and the socket circuit include:

(1)　the lighting circuit is in parallel; the socket circuit is ring main (but still in parallel),

(2)　the lighting circuit carries a maximum current of 5 A; the socket circuit carries a maximum current of 30 A,

(3)　with a smaller current, the lighting circuit uses thinner cable.

❑　The mains fuses protect the mains wiring; fuses prevent overheating from too large a current with risk of fire.

❑　A **circuit breaker** is an automatic switch which can be used instead of a fuse.

○　A circuit breaker is used instead of a fuse because it can quickly be switched back on and reused.

❑ The **kilowatt-hour**, kWh, is a unit of energy; it is used by electricity boards in costing electricity:

> **1 kWh = 1 kilowatt x 1 hour**

❑ When calculating the cost of electricity, power should be left in kilowatts and time in hours; **do not change to joules and seconds:**

> **Number of kWh = number of kW x number of hours**

❑ *Example*
What is the cost of using a 750 W drill continuously for 30 minutes, at 6 p per unit.

Step 1 Put the information into symbol form and change to basic units (kW and hours in this case)

P = 750 W = 0.75 kW
t = 30 mins = 0.5 h

Step 2 Choose the correct equation.

$E = Pt$

Step 3 Put the numbers into the equation and calculate the answer.

$E = Pt$ = 0.75 x 0.5 = 0.375 kWh

Step 4 Calculate the cost at 6 p per kWh.

Cost = 0.375 x 6 = **2.25 p**

DO NOT FORGET UNITS.

○ Since both kWh and J are units of energy they are related.

○ To find out how many joules in a kilowatt-hour change kW into W and hours into seconds:

> 1 kW = 1000 W   1 h = 60 x 60 s
>
> Therefore 1 kWh = 1000 x 60 x 60 J = 3 600 000 J

Section 6   Movement from electricity

❑   When there is a current in a wire, there is a magnetic field round the wire.

❑   When a wire carrying a current is placed in a magnetic field, there is a force on the wire.

❑   **Current, magnetic field** and **force** (or **movement**) are three related variables;
if two are present, the third will be produced.

○   The direction of the force depends on the direction of the current and the direction of the magnetic field; changing **either** the field or the current will change the direction of the force.

❑   The magnetic effect of the current is used in:

(1) electric bells,
(2) relays,
(3) electromagnets.

❑   **An electric motor**

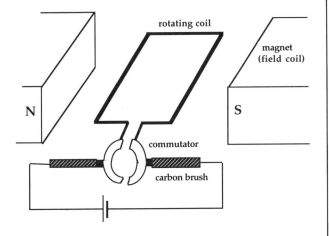

In a **d.c. motor:**

○ the rotating coil is carrying a current and since it is between the poles of a magnet, there is also a magnetic field;
therefore there is a force on the coil;
this force makes the coil turn but it will only continue to turn if the force always acts to turn it in the same direction;
in order to achieve this the current has to change direction every half turn;
the **commutator** does this.

○ the **brushes** make electrical contact with the commutator but still allow the coil to turn.

In a **commercial motor** there are:

○ **carbon brushes** to make contact;
carbon is used because it is a good conductor but soft enough to wear away as the commutator turns without damaging the commutator,

○ **field coils** to provide the magnetic field rather than a permanent magnet;
these are fixed coils which carry a current and become electromagnets;
these can provide a stronger magnetic field and are much lighter than permanent magnets,

○ **multi-section commutators;**
the force is greatest when the coil is at right angles to the magnetic field;
with a multi-section commutator one of the coils is always nearly at right angles and thus the force stays large and the rotation is much smoother.

UNIT 3   HEALTH PHYSICS

Section 1   **The use of thermometers**

❑   A **thermometer** requires some measurable physical property that changes with temperature.

❑   In a **thermocouple**, the voltage varies with temperature.

❑   In a **mercury in glass** thermometer, the volume of the mercury and hence the length of the column of mercury changes with temperature.

❑   **A clinical thermometer**

    (1) The thermometer has a constriction (kink); this makes the mercury thread break as it cools and contracts; the thread stays at the maximum temperature.

    (2) The thermometer measures only over a small range (35 - 43 °C); this is just above and below the body temperature of 37 °C.

    (3) A toughened glass tube with a shaped front acts as a lens to magnify the mercury thread.

❑   **Measuring body temperature**

    (1) Shake the thread down to make the mercury go back into the bowl.

    (2) Place the bowl under the tongue and leave for a few minutes.

    (3) Read the scale opposite the end of the mercury thread to give the temperature.

❑   Normal body temperature is 37 °C.

❑   If the temperature is above 37 °C, the person is feverish, usually due to some infection;
if the temperature is above 43 °C the person is close to death!

❑   If the temperature is below 34 °C, the person is suffering from **hypothermia**; if the temperature is below 28 °C the person is close to death!

Section 2   Using sound

❑   Sound is caused by **vibrations** and can only be transmitted when there are particles to vibrate; therefore sound travels through solids, liquids and gases but not through a vacuum.

❑   The **stethoscope** picks up sounds from the body and passes the vibrations along a column of air in the tube to the doctor's ears; the sounds are loudest when there is **resonance** between the skin and the bell.

❑   There are two bells in a stethoscope:
(1) an open bell for low frequency heart sounds,
(2) a closed bell for high frequency lung sounds.

❑   The normal range of human hearing is approximately 20 Hz to 20 000 Hz; sounds with frequencies above this range are called **ultrasounds.**

❑   Ultrasound is used to:
(1) examine a baby in the womb (safer than X-rays),
(2) break up kidney stones in the body (no surgery).

○   When used to examine the foetus, ultrasound is directed into the mother's body; a layer of jelly stops the skin reflecting the sound waves;
the waves reflect off the baby and these reflections are used to build up the image of the baby.

❑   **Noise levels** are measured in **decibels, dB**; typical noise levels are:

minimum sound that can be heard	0 dB
ordinary conversation	60 dB
heavy lorry	95 dB
pneumatic drill	100 dB
pop group at 1 m	110 dB
jet engine	130 dB
pain threshold	140 dB

❑   Regular exposure to noise above 90 dB can cause damage to hearing.

❑   Noise levels from 90 dB upwards are examples of noise pollution. *Learn at least two.*

Section 3   Light and sight

❑   **Refraction** of light occurs when light moves from one material into another and is usually accompanied by a change in direction. It is caused by a change in speed in the different materials.

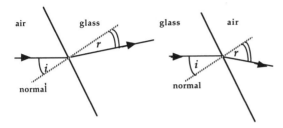

○   *i* is the angle of incidence;
    r is the angle of refraction;
    the **normal** is a construction line at right angles to the boundary at the point where the incident ray meets the boundary.

❑   There are two main shapes of lens:

   Convex (converging)   **Concave** (diverging)

❑   **The eye**

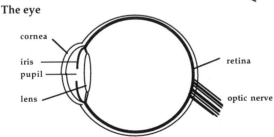

❑   Light is focused on the retina at the back of the eye by:

   (1) the cornea - most refraction takes place here,
   (2) the lens   - can change shape and gives fine control of focusing.

❑   The image formed on the retina is upside down (inverted) and back to front (laterally inverted).

❏ A ray diagram shows that an inverted image is formed on the retina:

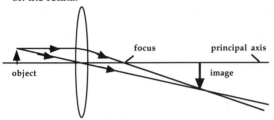

❏ The position of any image can be found by drawing two rays:

(1) a ray through the centre of the lens which does not change direction,
(2) a ray parallel to the principal axis which goes through the focus.

○ The lens in the eye can change shape; this is called **accommodation**.

○ Light rays coming from a **distant object** arrive at the eye parallel; the lens is **thin**:

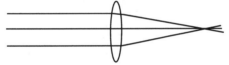

○ Light rays from a **nearby object** diverge; the lens is much **thicker**:

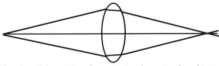

❏ The **focal length** of a convex lens is the distance between the lens and the point where parallel rays are brought to a focus; this can be measured experimentally by obtaining a clear image of a **distant** object, eg. the view from a window on a screen; the focal length is the distance between the lens and the screen.

❑ People can only see clearly if the light is focused on the retina.

❑ In **long sight**, light from nearby objects is focused behind the retina and only objects a long way away are clear.

❑ In **short sight**, light from distant objects is focused in front of the retina and only objects close at hand are clear.

❑ Both long and short sight can be corrected using lenses.

○ **Long sight**

Use of a convex lens causes light to converge more, so that it is focused on the retina:

○ **Short sight**

Use of a concave lens causes light to diverge before it enters the eye so that it is focused on the retina:

 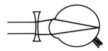

○ The **power** of a lens is measured in **dioptres, D.**

○ Power is related to focal length by the equation:

$$\text{power of lens} = \frac{1}{\text{focal length (in metres)}}$$

or

$$\text{focal length} = \frac{1}{\text{power}}$$

○ Both focal length and power are:

negative for **concave lens**
positive for **convex lens**

○   *Example*
A lens has a focal length of -25 cm. Find the power of
the lens and state whether it is concave or convex.

Step 1 Put the information into symbol form and
change to basic units.

f = -25 cm = -0.25 m

Step 2 Choose the correct equation.

$$\text{power} = \frac{1}{f}$$

Step 3 Put the numbers into the equation and
calculate the answer.

$$\text{power} = \frac{1}{f} = \frac{-1}{0.25} = \text{-4 D}$$

DO NOT FORGET UNITS.

Since the power is negative, it is a **concave** lens.

❑   **Fibre optics** can be used to transmit 'cold light';
since the source of the light can be a long way from the
tip of the fibre optic, only the light reaches the tip and
not the heat, ie. 'cold light'.

○   An **endoscope** (or fibroscope) consists of two bundles
of optical fibres;
the first bundle carries cold light down to the tip;
the second bundle has a lens at the tip and sends an
image back up the fibre optic;
the tube is flexible and can be moved around inside the
body to view the inside.

○   The light passes down the optical fibre by **total internal
reflection**.

Section 4   Using the spectrum

❑   A **laser** gives a very intense beam of light which carries
       a lot of energy;
       it act as a very sharp knife and seals blood vessels
       as it cuts.

❑   A laser can be used to:

       (1) remove birth marks,
       (2) remove tumours,
       (3) repair the retina.

❑   **X-rays** can be used to find broken bones;
       the bone is dense enough to absorb X-rays while the
       flesh lets X-rays through;
       this produces a 'shadow' picture of the bones, which
       appear pale, on a photographic plate;
       where there is a break, there is a dark line.

❑   Photographic film can be used to detect X-rays.

○   **Computerised tomography** takes a series of X-ray
       pictures of horizontal slices through the body;
       the X-ray tube rotates round the body to allow
       readings from all directions;
       the computer builds up a 3-D picture of the particular
       organ and can find very small changes;
       it allows tumours to be found while they are still small
       and the position accurately located so that they can be
       treated.

❑   **Infra red** (heat) radiation can be used to help heal
       strained muscles and tissues.

❑   Since tumours are slightly warmer than the
       surrounding tissue, thermograms which detect the infra
       red emitted by tissue, can be used to find tumours.

❑   **Ultra violet** can be used to treat skin problems;
       it is also used to sterilise instruments by killing bacteria.

❑   Ultra violet is the part of the sun's radiation which
       causes tanning, but too much can cause skin cancer.

Section 5   Nuclear radiation - humans and medicine

❑   Radiation can kill or change the nature of living cells.

❑   Radiation can be used to:

(1) sterilise instruments by killing germs,
(2) kill the cells which make up a cancerous tumour.

❑   Radioactive material can be detected by the radiation it gives off;
usually gamma radiation is used in medicine since it can be detected outside the body.

❑   A **tracer** is a radioactive substance which is either injected into the body or swallowed;
the tracer is concentrated in the organ the doctor wishes to examine and the movement of the tracer is measured by the gamma radiation,
eg. tracers can be used to study the uptake of iodine by the thyroid gland.

❑   The energy carried by radiation can be absorbed by the material it is passing through.

❑   There are three types of radiation:

alpha - α
beta - β
gamma - γ

❑   These three radiations can be identified by their different absorption properties.

❑   The source is placed in front of a Geiger-Muller tube and the amount of radiation passing through the absorber registers on the scaler;

various absorbers can be used:

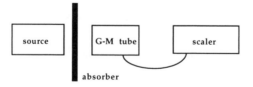

❑ Alpha radiation is absorbed by paper;
beta radiation is absorbed by a few millimetres of
aluminium;
gamma radiation is absorbed by a few centimetres of
lead.

❑ Alpha radiation is absorbed by a few centimetres of air;
beta radiation is absorbed by a few metres of air;
gamma radiation is not absorbed by air.

❑ The atom consists of a central **nucleus** with orbiting
electrons.

❑ The nucleus contains positively charged **protons** and
uncharged **neutrons**;
it has nearly all of the mass of the atom and all the
positive charge.

❑ The electrons are negatively charged and much lighter
(1/2000 th) than neutrons or protons:

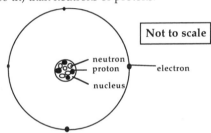

○ An atom is normally electrically neutral as it has the
same number of negative electrons orbiting the atom
as positive protons in the nucleus.

○ **Ionisation** occurs when the atom gains an electron to
give it an overall negative charge, or loses an electron
to give it an overall positive charge.

❑ When radiation passes through a material it can ionise
the atoms of that material.

❑ Alpha rays produce much more ionisation than beta or
gamma.

❑ Radiation will fog photographic plates.

○ This is used in film badges;
various parts of the film are covered by different
thicknesses of various absorbers;
when the badge is developed, the film will only be
affected if radiation has passed through the absorber;
by examining which areas are affected, the type and
amount of radiation can be determined.

☐ Radiation is absorbed by some materials and the energy re-emitted as light, called **scintillations**.

○ This effect is used in scintillation counters and gamma cameras.

○ Ionisation takes place in the Geiger-Muller tube:

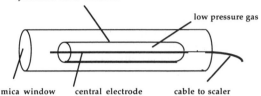

cylindrical outer electrode

low pressure gas

mica window   **central electrode**   **cable to scaler**

○ A current cannot normally pass between the central electrode and the cylindrical outer electrode, but when the gas becomes ionised it allows a current to pass; this pulse of current is measured on the scaler; the window is very thin mica to allow even alpha particles into the tube.

☐ The **activity** of a radioactive source is measured in **becquerels, Bq**, where one becquerel is one atom decaying per second.

☐ The activity of a radioactive source decreases with time.

☐ Safety precautions for handling radioactive material include:

(1) always use forceps to handle sources,
(2) make sure the source is never pointed at anyone,
(3) store in lead-lined boxes,
(4) label all radioactive material.

○ The biological effect of radiation depends on:

(1) the type of radiation,
(2) the type of body tissue which absorbs it,
(3) the total amount of energy absorbed.

☐ The **dose equivalent** is measured in **sieverts, Sv.**

○ The dose equivalent takes into account the type and energy of the radiation.

○ The decay of an individual atom is a totally random event and cannot be predicted.

○ However the time taken for half the atoms, in a sample of a particular radioactive material, to decay is always the same;
this is called the **half life.**

○ The half life is the time taken for the activity of a sample to drop by half.

○ The half life can be found from an Activity/Time graph; this is obtained by placing the source in front of a Geiger-Muller tube, measuring the activity every minute and plotting the results:

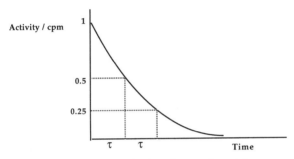

The initial activity is marked on the graph and then a line parallel to the time axis is drawn at half this activity;
from the point where the line meets the curve, a line parallel to the activity axis is drawn;
the half life is given by the point where the line cuts the time axis.

○ Any initial activity can be chosen;
the half life will always be the same for a given radioactive material.

There are two main types of problem involving half life:

○ **Example 1**
If a source of activity 4000 kBq has a half life of 3 days, what is its activity 18 days later?

Number of half lives = $\dfrac{\text{Number of days}}{\text{Half life in days}}$ = $\dfrac{18}{3}$ = 6

4000 → 2000 → 1000 → 500 → 250 → 125 → 62.5
    1τ   2τ   3τ   4τ   5τ   6τ

The activity after 18 days is **62.5 kBq.**

○ **Example 2**
If a source of activity 1600 kBq has dropped to an activity of 200 kBq in 30 days, what is the half life of the source?

1600 → 800 → 400 → 200
     1τ   2τ   3τ

The number of half lives is 3.

Half life in days = $\dfrac{\text{Number of days}}{\text{Number of half lives}}$

= $\dfrac{30}{3}$

= 10

The half life is **10 days.**

UNIT 4   ELECTRONICS

Section 1   Overview

❏ An electronic system consists of three parts:

INPUT → PROCESS → OUTPUT

❏ There are two types of output:

> **digital**
> **analogue**

❏ In a digital output, the system can only be at particular levels, often in only two states, ie. either ON or OFF;
in an analogue output, there is a continuously varying value.

❏ On an oscilloscope these give:

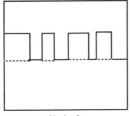 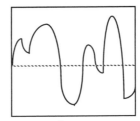

digital   **analogue**

Section 2   Output devices

❑   In each case the main energy change is from electrical to some other form:

Device	Output energy	Analogue or digital
Motor	kinetic (rotation)	analogue
Solenoid	kinetic (in straight line)	digital
Buzzer	sound	digital
Loudspeaker	sound	analogue
LED	light	digital
Relay	kinetic	digital
7-segment display	light	digital

○   **Choosing the correct output device for a given situation**

(1) Decide what form of energy is required to be given out.
(2) Where appropriate, decide whether a digital or an analogue device would be better.

❑   The symbol for an **LED (light emitting diode)** is:

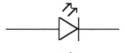

direction of electron flow

❑   An LED will only allow current through it in one direction;
therefore it only lights when connected the correct way round.

❑   An LED will be damaged if too large a current passes through it;
a series resistor limits the size of the current so that the LED is not damaged.

○ The following circuit will allow the LED to light:

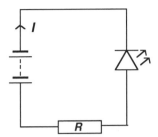

The value of the series resistor required for a given LED and given supply can be calculated.

Example
○ If the LED takes 10 mA and 2 V to work correctly, calculate the series resistor required with a 5 V supply.

Step 1 As the supply voltage is 5 V and the LED requires 2 V, the voltage across the series resistor is:

5 - 2 = 3 V

(Voltages in series add up to the supply voltage.)

Step 2 Change the current through the series resistor to basic units.

I = 10 mA = 0.01 A

(The current is the same at all points in a series circuit.)

Step 3 Calculate the resistance using Ohm's law.

$$V = IR \Rightarrow R = \frac{V}{I} = \frac{3}{0.01} = 300 \ \Omega$$

DO NOT FORGET UNITS.

❑ A 7-segment display consists of seven bars (LEDs) which can be lit up independently.

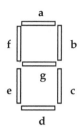

a

f   b

g

e   c

d

Digit	Segments lit
0	abcdef
1	bc
2	abged
3	abcdg
4	fgbc
5	afgcd
6	afecdg
7	abc or abcf
8	abcdefg
9	abcdfg or abcfg

Do not bother to learn;
look at the display on the calculator.

○ A binary number is expressed in terms of '0' or '1' only;
the positions of the '1's give its value.

8	4	2	1	Decimal number
0	0	0	0	0
0	0	0	1	1
0	0	1	0	2
0	0	1	1	3
0	1	0	0	4
0	1	0	1	5
0	1	1	0	6
0	1	1	1	7
1	0	0	0	8
1	0	0	1	9

Section 3   Input devices

❑   A **microphone**, symbol ⬭ ,   changes
    sound energy into electrical energy.

❑   A **thermocouple**, symbol -⤵+ , changes
    heat into electrical energy.

❑   A **solar cell** changes light energy into electrical
    energy.

❑   A **thermistor**, symbol ⟝⟍⟞ , is a
    resistor the resistance of which varies with
    temperature;
    as the temperature increases, resistance decreases.

❑   An **LDR**, symbol ⟝▭⟞ , is a light
    dependent resistor;
    as the light intensity increases, the resistance
    decreases.

❑   Ohm's law, $V = I R$, can be used to calculate the
    resistance of either a thermistor or an LDR.

❑   A **capacitor**, symbol ⟝⟝ , stores energy and
    charge.

❑   As a capacitor becomes charged the voltage across it
    increases;
    this does not happen instantaneously:

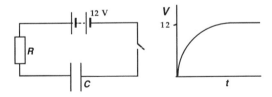

◯   The voltage increases up to the supply voltage;
    the time it takes to do so depends on the values of the
    capacitor **C** and the resistor **R**.

◯   Increasing **C** or increasing **R** (or both) increases the
    time.

○ **Choosing the correct input device for a given situation**

(1) For anything involving a time delay use a capacitor and resistor.
(2) In other cases look at the form of energy providing the information and choose the appropriate device,
eg. for temperature changes (heat) use a thermistor.

○ **Voltage dividers**

Resistors can be used to split the supply voltage:

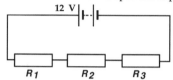

Total resistance $R_T = R_1 + R_2 + R_3$

Voltage across $R_1 = \dfrac{R_1}{R_1 + R_2 + R_3}$ x supply voltage

○ *Example*

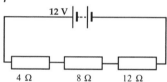

Total resistance $= 4 + 8 + 12 = 24\,\Omega$

Voltage across $4\,\Omega = \dfrac{4}{24} \times 12 = 2\,V$

Voltage across $8\,\Omega = \dfrac{8}{24} \times 12 = 4\,V$

Voltage across $12\,\Omega = \dfrac{12}{24} \times 12 = 6\,V$

Section 4   Digital processes

❑   A **transistor** can be used as a switch.

❑   A transistor can be either ON or OFF, ie. it either
     conducts and allows a current through it or it does
     not.

❑   The symbol for an NPN transistor is:

where   **b** is the base
         e is the emitter
         c is the collector.

Switching circuits

❑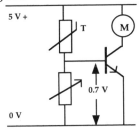

The circuit switches the motor on when it gets hot.

◯   For the transistor to switch on, there must be 0.7 V
     across the base - emitter junction;
     as the thermistor heats up its resistance decreases so
     the voltage across it decreases;
     the voltage across the variable resistor increases to
     more than 0.7 V and the transistor switches on.

❑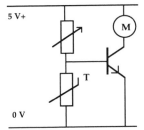

**The circuit switches the motor off when it gets hot or
it switches the motor on when it gets cold.**

○ As the thermistor heats up its resistance decreases so the voltage across it falls below 0.7 V and the transistor switches off.

❑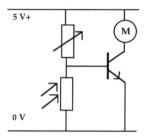

The circuit switches the motor on when it gets dark.

○ As light intensity falls the resistance of the LDR increases;
the voltage across the LDR increases to more than 0.7 V;
the transistor switches the motor on.

❑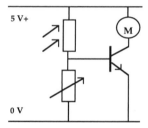

The circuit switches the motor on when it gets light.

○ As light intensity increases the LDR has lower resistance and less voltage across it;
therefore the voltage across the variable resistor increases to more than 0.7 V and the transistor switches the motor on.

○ In each of the previous circuits the variable resistor is present to allow the exact point at which the transistor switches to be adjusted.

○ **Time delay circuit**

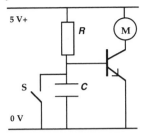

With **S** open the capacitor slowly charges up and the voltage across it increases;
when the voltage reaches 0.7 V the transistor switches the motor on;
since the capacitor takes time to charge up there is a delay between switching 'on', ie. opening the switch, and the motor coming on;
the length of the delay can be increased by increasing the value of **R** or **C**;
S is there to discharge the capacitor so that it is ready to use again.

Logic gates

❑ The symbols are:

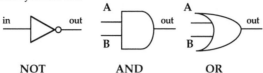

NOT   **AND**   **OR**

(an inverter)

❑ High voltage = logic '**1**';
low voltage = logic '**0**'.

❑ Logic gates can have one or more inputs.

❑ Truth tables show the output for all possible combinations of inputs.

❑ **NOT** gate

INPUT	OUTPUT
0	1
1	0

❑ **AND** gate

A	B	OUTPUT
0	0	0
0	1	0
1	0	0
1	1	1

❑ **OR** gate

A	B	OUTPUT
0	0	0
0	1	1
1	0	1
1	1	1

❑ Several logic gates can be combined to give the control required in a particular situation; the wording of a question can give a clue as to whether **AND** or **OR** gates are required, eg. dark can be thought of as **NOT** light, cold as **NOT** hot.

○   A truth table can be drawn up for combinations of
    gates.

Example

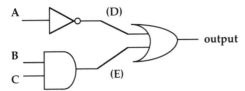

Step 1   Put all possible combinations of inputs **A,**
            B, C into the truth table.

Step 2   Work out logic states of **D** and **E.**
            (These do not necessarily have to be
            included in the truth table.)

Step 3   Work out logic state of output.

A	B	C	(D)	(E)	OUTPUT
0	0	0	1	0	1
0	1	0	1	0	1
0	0	1	1	0	1
0	1	1	1	1	1
1	0	0	0	0	0
1	1	0	0	0	0
1	0	1	0	0	0
1	1	1	0	1	1

❑   A digital circuit can produce a series of clock pulses.

❑   A digital circuit can count digital pulses.

❑   The output of these counter circuits is in binary.

❑   There are circuits which will change the binary output
    into decimal.

❑   Examples of devices containing a counter circuit are
    digital watches or calculators.

○ A **clock pulse generator** can be made from a resistor, capacitor and inverter:

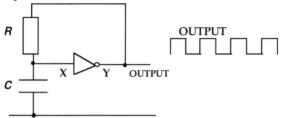

At the start, when the circuit is switched on, the capacitor is uncharged, so the voltage at **X** is low;
X is logic **0**;
Y is logic **1** and its voltage is 5 V;
as the capacitor charges, the voltage at **X** becomes high;
X becomes logic **1**;
Y is logic **0** and its voltage becomes 0 V;
the capacitor discharges through the resistor **R** until the voltage at **X** becomes low again;
the cycle repeats;
the output is a series of **high** and **low**.

○ The frequency of the clock can be changed by varying the values of **C** and **R** :

low values **C** and/or **R**   high values **C** and/or **R**

Section 5　　　Analogue processes

❑　An **amplifier** increases the strength of an electrical signal.

❑　The output signal from an amplifier has the same frequency but a larger amplitude than the input signal.

❑　Amplifiers are used in:
   (1)　radios and televisions,
   (2)　HiFi systems,
   (3)　baby alarms,
   (4)　many other systems where the detector (of heat, light, pressure, etc.) produces a small voltage.

❑　The **voltage gain** of an amplifier is given by:

$$\text{voltage gain} \quad = \quad \frac{\textbf{output voltage}}{\textbf{input voltage}}$$

❑　*Example*
　　What will be the output voltage of an amplifier with a gain of 90, when the input voltage is 5 mV?

Step 1　Put the information into symbol form and change to basic units.

　　　　　voltage gain = 90
　　　　　input voltage = 5 mV = 0.005 V

Step 2　Choose the correct equation.

$$\text{voltage gain} \quad = \quad \frac{\textbf{output voltage}}{\textbf{input voltage}} \quad =>$$

output voltage = voltage gain x input voltage

Step 3　Put the numbers into the equation and calculate the answer.

output voltage = voltage gain x input voltage

$$= 90 \times 0.005 \ = \ \textbf{0.45 V}$$

DO NOT FORGET UNITS.

○ An oscilloscope can be used to find the voltage gain of an amplifier:

(1) Measure the input voltage to the amplifier.
(2) Measure the output voltage of the amplifier.
(3) Use the voltage gain equation to calculate gain.

○ Power is related to voltage and resistance by the equation:

$$P = \frac{V^2}{R}$$

where P is the power in W
R is the resistance in Ω
V is the voltage in V

○ The power gain is given by:

$$\text{power gain} = \frac{\text{output power}}{\text{input power}}$$

○ **Example**
An amplifier has an output power of 50 W. If the input resistance is 1000 Ω and the input voltage is 12 V, calculate the power gain.

Step 1 Put the information into symbol form.

input resistance	=	1000 Ω
input voltage	=	12 V
output power	=	50 W

Step 2 Choose the correct equations.

$$P = \frac{V^2}{R}$$

$$\text{power gain} = \frac{\text{output power}}{\text{input power}}$$

Step 3 Put the numbers into the equations and calculate the answer.

$$P = \frac{V^2}{R} = \frac{12 \times 12}{1000} = 0.144 \text{ W}$$

$$\text{power gain} = \frac{\text{output power}}{\text{input power}} = \frac{50}{0.144} = 34.7$$

There are no units since power gain is a ratio.

UNIT 5   TRANSPORT

Section 1   On the move

❑   **Average speed** has the symbol $\overline{v}$, and is measured in metres per second, **m s^{-1}**.

❑   Average speed is given by:

$$\overline{v} = \frac{d}{t}$$

where **d** is the distance in m
         t is the time in s

Example
What is the average speed of an athlete who runs 100 m in 12.2 s?

Step 1   Put the information into symbol form.

   d = 100 m
   t = 12.2 s

Step 2   Choose the correct equation.

$$\overline{v} = \frac{d}{t}$$

Step 3   Put the numbers into the equation and calculate the answer.

$$\overline{v} = \frac{d}{t} = \frac{100}{12.2} = 8.20 \text{ m s}^{-1}$$

DO NOT FORGET UNITS.

Measuring average speed

❑   A distance, **d**, is measured out and then the object is timed from the start to the finish (**t**); the equation $\overline{v} = \frac{d}{t}$ is used to calculate the average speed; to increase accuracy, several repeat measurements of time are taken and an average is found.

❑   The instantaneous speed is the speed at one particular point in time and can be very different from the average speed.

○ A car travelling round town could be travelling at 30 m.p.h. and then be stationary at traffic lights; its average speed, for example, could be 12 m.p.h. which is different from the instantaneous speeds.

Measuring the instantaneous speed

❑ The time interval must be as short as possible; a light gate connected to an electronic timer will achieve this; when a card attached to the moving object breaks a light beam in the light gate, the timer starts; as soon as the beam is remade the timer stops; the speed can be calculated by:

$$\text{speed} = \frac{\text{length of card}}{\text{time beam is broken}}$$

○ The shorter the time interval, the closer this average speed comes to the instantaneous speed.

○ Any method of measuring time which involves a stop watch is inaccurate because of the reaction time of the person using the stopwatch.

❑ Speed is how fast an object is travelling and is numerically equal to the distance travelled in one second.

❑ **Acceleration** is the increase in speed in one second; it has the symbol a, and is measured in $m\ s^{-2}$.

❑ Acceleration is given by:

$$a = \frac{v - u}{t}$$

where u is the initial speed in $m\ s^{-1}$
v is the final speed in $m\ s^{-1}$
t is the time in s

❑ If the two speeds are given in m.p.h. and the time in seconds, then the acceleration will be in miles per hour per second.

❑ *Example*

What is the acceleration of a trolley which starts at 6.5 m s^{-1} and is travelling at 50 cm s^{-1} after 3 s?

Step 1 Put the information into symbol form and change to basic units.

$$u = 6.5 \text{ m s}^{-1}$$
$$v = 50 \text{ cm s}^{-1} = 0.5 \text{ m s}^{-1}$$
$$t = 3 \text{ s}$$

Step 2 Choose the correct equation.

$$a = \frac{v - u}{t}$$

Step 3 Put the numbers into the equation and calculate the answer.

$$a = \frac{v - u}{t} = \frac{0.5 - 6.5}{3} = \frac{-6}{3} = \textbf{-2 m s}^{-2}$$

DO NOT FORGET UNITS.

❑ The negative sign shows that this is a deceleration, i.e. the trolley is slowing down.

Speed - time graphs

You must be able to draw and recognise the following graphs.

☐ Steady speed

☐ Speeding up (Accelerating)

☐ Slowing down (Decelerating)

The information from a speed - time graph can be used to calculate:

☐ (1) the **acceleration**

using $a = \dfrac{v - u}{t}$,

○ (2) the **distance travelled**

which is equal to the **area** under a speed - time graph,

○ (3) the **maximum acceleration**

by calculating all accelerations and choosing the largest, or using the line with the steepest gradient.

Example

Use the following graph to

❑   (a) describe the motion,

❑   (b) calculate all accelerations,

❑   (c) state the maximum speed achieved,

⭕   (d) calculate the distance travelled.

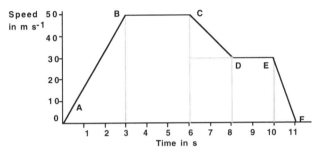

(a) AB - accelerating from rest to 50 m s^{-1} in 3 s

     BC - constant speed of 50 m s^{-1} for 3 s

     CD - decelerating from 50 m s^{-1} to 30 m s^{-1} in 2 s

     DE - constant speed of 30 m s^{-1} for 2 s

     EF - decelerating from 30 m s^{-1} to rest in 1 s

(b) AB $a = \dfrac{v - u}{t}$ $= \dfrac{50 - 0}{3}$ $= \;\; 16.7$ m s^{-2}

     CD $a = \dfrac{v - u}{t}$ $= \dfrac{30 - 50}{2}$ $= -10$ m s^{-2}

     EF $a = \dfrac{v - u}{t}$ $= \dfrac{0 - 30}{1}$ $= -30$ m s^{-2}

(c) Maximum speed $= 50$ m s^{-1}

(d) Distance travelled = area under the graph

     AB $= \;\; \frac{1}{2}(3 \times 50)$ $= \;\; 75$ m

     BC $= \;\; (3 \times 50)$ $= \;\; 150$ m

     CD $= \;\; \frac{1}{2}[(50 - 30) \times 2] + [2 \times 30] = 20 + 60 \;\; = \;\; 80$ m

     DE $= \;\; (2 \times 30)$ $= \;\; 60$ m

     EF $= \;\; \frac{1}{2}(30 \times 1)$ $= \;\; \underline{15\text{ m}}$

                          Total distance $= \;\; 380$ m

○ The acceleration formula can be rewritten:

$$v = u + at$$

where
v is the final speed in m s^{-1}
u is the initial speed in m s^{-1}
a is the acceleration in m s^{-2}
t is the time in s

○ *Example*
If a trolley accelerates from rest at 50 cm s^{-2} for 15 s, what is the final speed?

Step 1 Put the information into symbol form and change to basic units.

u = 0
a = 50 cm s^{-2} = 0.5 m s^{-2}
t = 15 s

Step 2 Choose the correct equation.

$v = u + at$

Step 3 Put the numbers into the equation and calculate the answer.

$v = u + at$
= 0 + 0.5 x 15 = **7.5 m s^{-1}**

DO NOT FORGET UNITS.

Section 2   Forces at work

❏   **Force** has the symbol **F**, and is measured in newtons, **N**.

❏   A force can change:

(1) the shape of an object,
(2) the speed of an object,
(3) the direction in which an object is moving.

❏   A **Newton balance** (or spring balance) is used to measure force.

❏   The Newton balance contains a spring;
the spring becomes longer when a force is applied to the balance;
the increase in length is directly proportional to the force.

❏   **Weight** is a force and is measured in newtons.

❏   The weight of an object is the Earth's pull on the object.

❏   The **mass** of an object is the amount of matter in the object.

○   The mass of an object does not change but the weight depends on the gravitational field strength and can vary.

○   The weight per unit mass is called the **gravitational field strength**;
it has the symbol **g** , and is measured in newtons per kilogram, **N kg^{-1}**.

$$g = \frac{W}{m}$$

where   **W**   is the weight in N
        m   is the mass in kg

❏   The approximate value of **g** is **10 N kg^{-1}** on Earth.

❏   The acceleration due to gravity is numerically equal to the gravitational field strength,
eg. on Earth, **g** = 10 N kg^{-1} and the acceleration due to gravity is 10 m s^{-2}.

❑ The relationship between gravitational field strength, weight and mass can be rewritten:

$$W = m\,g$$

where W is the weight in N
m is the mass in kg
g is 10 N kg^{-1} (on Earth)

❑ *Example*
On Earth, what is the weight of a man of mass 70 kg?

Step 1 Put the information into symbol form.

m = 70 kg
g = 10 N kg^{-1}

Step 2 Choose the correct equation.

$$W = m\,g$$

Step 3 Put the numbers into the equation and calculate the answer.

$$W = m\,g = 70 \times 10 = 700\ \text{N}$$

DO NOT FORGET UNITS.

❑ **Friction** is a force which can oppose the motion of a body.

❑ Friction is **increased** by:

(1) applying brakes,
(2) opening a parachute; there is more air resistance so that the person falls more slowly,
(3) using aerofoils on racing cars; the aerofoils hold the car down and allow faster cornering.

❑ Friction is **decreased** by:

(1) using oil between moving parts in machinery,
(2) making objects streamlined,
(3) reducing the area of contact, eg. using wheels or rollers,
(4) making surfaces smooth, eg. wax on skis.

❑ The direction of a force is important.

❑ If the forces acting in opposite directions are equal, they are called **balanced forces**, eg.

F ←[ ]→ F   ↑F [ ] ↓F   F →[ ]← F

❑ Balanced forces have the same effect on motion as having no force at all.

❑ When the forces are balanced or there are no forces, the speed remains constant.

❑ When an object is moving at a constant speed, the forces on it are either balanced or zero.

○ **Newton's First Law** states that an object remains at rest or continues in the same direction at the same speed, unless there is an unbalanced force acting.

○ The motion of a spaceship is consistent with Newton's First Law;
space is a vacuum so there are no frictional forces acting;
the spaceship continues moving at the same speed in the same direction until it comes under the gravitational influence of a planet.

❑ Seat belts are used in cars to provide a backwards force to prevent the passenger continuing to move forward if the car stops suddenly;
if there was no such force, from Newton's First Law, the passenger would continue moving forward at the original speed of the car and may go through the windscreen.

❑ **Newton's Second Law** states that:

$$F = m a$$

where F is the force in N
m is the mass in kg
a is the acc. in m s^{-2}

❑ The unbalanced or resultant force must be used for F in the above equation.

❑ When the force stays the same and the mass increases, the acceleration decreases.

❑ When the mass stays the same and the force increases, the acceleration increases.

❑   *Example 1*
What is the mass of an object if an unbalanced force
of 20 N produces an acceleration of 4 m s^{-2}?

Step 1   Put the information into symbol form.

$$F = 20\,N$$
$$a = 4\,m\,s^{-2}$$

Step 2   Choose the correct equation.

$$F = ma \quad => \quad m = \frac{F}{a}$$

Step 3   Put the numbers into the equation and
calculate the answer.

$$m = \frac{F}{a} = \frac{20}{4} = 5\,kg$$

DO NOT FORGET UNITS.

○ *Example 2*

What is the acceleration of a 600 kg car, when the engine exerts a force of 1700 N, but the frictional force is 800 N?

Step 1   Draw a simple diagram showing the forces acting and their directions.

800 N ◄━┤ 600 kg ├━► 1700 N

Step 2   Calculate the resultant (unbalanced) force.

$$F = 1700 - 800 = 900 \text{ N}$$

┌─────────┐
│ 600 kg ├━► 900 N
└─────────┘

Step 3   Put the information into symbol form.

$$F = 900 \text{ N}$$
$$m = 600 \text{ kg}$$

Step 4   Choose the correct equation.

$$F = ma \quad => \quad a = \frac{F}{m}$$

Step 5   Put the numbers into the equation and calculate the answer.

$$a = \frac{F}{m} = \frac{900}{600} = 1.5 \text{ m s}^{-2}$$

DO NOT FORGET UNITS.

❑   The two equations:

$$a = \frac{F}{m} \quad \text{and} \quad a = \frac{v - u}{t}$$

can be used to calculate the acceleration.

Choose the correct equation for the information given; often both equations are used in same question.

Section 3   Movement means energy

❏   Energy can be changed from one form into another (energy transformations) but it cannot be created or destroyed;
energy is always conserved.

❏   All forms of energy can be measured in joules, **J**.

❏   Some examples of energy transformations:

(1) Car is accelerating

Chemical energy -> Kinetic energy + Heat

(2) Car moving at constant speed

Chemical energy -> Heat (E_k stays constant)

(3) Car braking

Kinetic energy -> Heat

(4) Car moving uphill at constant speed

Chemical energy -> Potential energy + Heat

(5) Car rolling downhill

Potential energy -> Kinetic energy + Heat

❏   In many transformations energy is 'lost' as heat due to friction.

❏   The **work done** is a measure of the energy transferred;
it has the symbol E_w , and is measured in joules, **J**

❏   Work done is related to force and distance by the equation:

$$\boxed{E_w = F\,d}$$
     where **F** is the force in N
                 d is the distance in m

❑ *Example*
How far must a 5 N force have pulled a 50 g toy car if 30 J of energy are transferred?

Step 1 Put the information into symbol form and change to basic units.

$$F = 5\,N$$
$$m = 50\,g = 0.05\,kg$$
$$E = 30\,J$$

(The mass is extra unnecessary information.)

Step 2 Choose the correct equation.

$$E_W = F\,d \quad \Rightarrow \quad d = \frac{E_W}{F}$$

Step 3 Put the numbers into the equation and calculate the answer.

$$d = \frac{E_W}{F} = \frac{30}{5} = 6\,m$$

DO NOT FORGET UNITS.

In certain calculations you do not always need to use all the information given.

❑ **Power** has the symbol *P*, and is measured in watts, **W**; one watt is one joule per second:

$$1\,W = 1\,J\,s^{-1}$$

❑ Power is related to energy and time by the equation:

$$\boxed{P = \frac{E}{t}}$$ where *E* is the energy in J
  t is the time in s

❑ This general equation is true when the energy involved is work done, ie. $E = E_W$.

❑ *Example*
What is the power of a cyclist who exerts a force of
50 N and moves 3 km in 10 minutes?

Step 1 Put the information into symbol form and
change to basic units.

F = 50 N
d = 3 km = 3000 m
t = 10 mins = 600 s

Step 2 Choose the correct equations.

$$E_w = F d$$

$$P = \frac{E}{t}$$

Step 3 Put the numbers into the equations and
calculate the answer.

$$E_w = F d = 50 \times 3000 = 150\,000 \text{ J}$$

$$P = \frac{E}{t} = \frac{150\,000}{600} = 250 \text{ W}$$

DO NOT FORGET UNITS.

*In certain calculations two equations have to be used to
find the answer.*

○ The work done against gravity is the **gravitational
potential energy;**
it has the symbol E_p and is measured in joules, **J**.

❑ $\boxed{E_p = m g h}$ where m is the mass in kg
g is the acceleration due to
gravity, 10 m s^{-2}
h is the vertical height in m

❑ The change in gravitational potential energy is the
work done against or by gravity.

❑ **Kinetic energy** is the energy an object has because it
is moving;
it has the symbol E_k, and is measured in joules, **J**.

❑ When the mass of the moving object is increased E_k
increases.

❏ When the speed of the moving object is increased E_k increases.

○ $$E_k = \frac{1}{2} m v^2$$ where E_k is the kinetic energy in J
    m is the mass in kg
    v is the speed in m s^{-1}

○ To find the speed given the kinetic energy and the mass, use the equation:

$$v = \sqrt{\frac{2 E_k}{m}}$$

○ *Example*
    What is the kinetic energy of a 3 kg trolley moving at 80 cm s^{-1}?

    Step 1 Put the information into symbol form and change to basic units.

    $m = 3$ kg
    $v = 80$ cm s^{-1} $= 0.8$ m s^{-1}

    Step 2 Choose the correct equation.

    $$E_k = \frac{1}{2} m v^2$$

    Step 3 Put the numbers into the equation and calculate the answer.

    $$E_k = \frac{1}{2} m v^2 = \frac{1}{2} \times 3 \times (0.8)^2 = 0.96 \text{ J}$$

    (Note that it is only the speed which is squared.)

    DO NOT FORGET UNITS.

○ Since energy is conserved, if it is possible to calculate the total energy at any one point, then the total energy is known at every other point.

Example

A 250 g pendulum bob is raised 20 cm
from its rest position and released.
(a) What is the potential energy at **A**?
(b) What is the kinetic energy at **B**?
(c) How fast is it travelling at **B**?

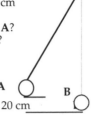

A   **B**

20 cm

Step 1 Put the information into symbol form and
change to basic units.

$$m = 250 \text{ g} = 0.25 \text{ kg}$$
$$h = 20 \text{ cm} = 0.2 \text{ m}$$
$$g = 10 \text{ m s}^{-2}$$

(a)

Step 2 Choose the correct equation.

$$E_p = m g h$$

Step 3 Put the numbers into the equation and
calculate the answer.

$$E_p = m g h = 0.25 \times 10 \times 0.2 = 0.5 \text{ J}$$

(b) $E_k = E_p$ (Energy is conserved.)

$$E_k = 0.5 \text{ J}$$

(c)

Step 2 Choose the correct equation.

$$E_k = \frac{1}{2} m v^2 \quad => \quad v = \sqrt{\frac{2 E_k}{m}}$$

Step 3 Put the numbers into the equation and
calculate the answer.

$$v = \sqrt{\frac{2 E_k}{m}} = \sqrt{\frac{2 \times 0.5}{0.25}} = \sqrt{4} = 2 \text{ m s}^{-1}$$

DO NOT FORGET UNITS.

○ Since the formulae for both E_k and E_p contain the mass, the speed or the height can be calculated, given the other, without needing to know the mass:

$$E_p = E_k$$
$$mgh = \frac{1}{2}mv^2$$

The mass can be cancelled from both sides:

$$gh = \frac{1}{2}v^2$$

This can be written as:

$$\boxed{v = \sqrt{2gh}}$$

○ *Example*
A man kicks a ball off a cliff which is 125 m high.
(a) How fast is it travelling vertically just before it hits the ground?
(b) What assumption is being made to obtain the answer?

(a)
Step 1 Put the information into symbol form.

$$h = 125\,\text{m}$$
$$g = 10\,\text{m s}^{-2}$$

(This is not stated in the question but is always true for vertical movement.)

Step 2 Choose the correct equation.

$$v = \sqrt{2gh}$$

Step 3 Put the numbers into the equation and calculate the answer.

$$v = \sqrt{2gh} = \sqrt{2 \times 10 \times 125} = 50\,\text{m s}^{-1}$$

DO NOT FORGET UNITS.

(b) The assumption made is that no energy is lost; all the potential energy becomes kinetic energy.

○ In practice, some energy is always 'lost' as heat; so the value obtained for the speed is therefore a maximum possible value.

UNIT 6   ENERGY MATTERS

Section 1   Supply and demand

❑   **Fossil fuels** are the main source of energy at present.

❑   Fossil fuels are the highly compressed remains of plants and animals after millions of years.

❑   The reserves of fossil fuels are **finite**, ie. they will eventually run out.

❑   Energy can be transformed from one form into another.

Energy can be "conserved", ie. saved

❑   (1) **in the home by**:
using insulation,
turning down the temperature,
switching off unwanted lights and appliances.

❑   (2) **in industry by**:
switching off unwanted appliances,
turning down the temperature,
using fans to circulate heat,
insulating.

❑   (3) **in transport by**:
using public transport,
carrying more people in each car,
limiting the speed,
taking more care on driving
    (less acceleration, braking, etc.).

❑   Energy sources are classified as renewable (alternative sources) and non-renewable:

Renewable	Non-renewable
solar	coal
wind	oil
waves	gas
tidal	peat
geothermal	uranium
hydroelectric	

○ **Advantages of renewable sources**

All are clean and renewable, ie. will not run out;
fuel is cheap (but may be expensive to collect).

Disadvantages of renewable sources

○ (1) **Solar**
The sun is not always shining;
solar panels have to be clean;
installations are expensive;
panels take up a lot of room for large amounts
of energy.

○ (2) **Wind**
The wind is not always blowing;
windmills can be an eyesore;
windmills take up a large amount of land.

○ (3) **Waves**
Waves are very variable in size;
the energy is provided a long way from where
it is required;
equipment is expensive
there are problems with ships using the same area.

○ (4) **Tidal**
There are only a few suitable locations.

○ (5) **Geothermal**
There are only a few suitable locations;
in less suitable places it is necessary to drill very deep;
this makes the energy expensive to obtain.

Section 2   Generation of electricity

❑   In a **thermal power station,** the energy transformations are:

   (1) in the boiler   -   chemical to heat
   (2) in the turbine   -   heat to work
   (3) in the generator   -   work to electrical

❑   The chemical energy can come from any fuel,
     e.g. coal, oil or gas.

❑   In a **hydroelectric power station,** the forms of
     energy involved are:

   (1) water behind the dam   -   has potential energy
   (2) water at the bottom   -   doing work
   (3) generator   -   generates electricity

❑   A **pumped hydroelectric scheme** is one where the
     water is pumped back into the reservoir behind the
     dam during the night when there is spare electricity;
     at this time demand is low and electricity is still being
     produced at the same rate.

❑   Pumping the water back is a way of storing the
     energy;
     the water can then be allowed to flow back down
     and produce electricity rapidly at the time of peak
     demand, eg. at meal times during the day.

❑   In a **nuclear power station**, the energy transformations
     are:

   (1) in the nuclear reactor   -   nuclear to heat
   (2) in the turbine   -   heat to work
   (3) in the generator   -   work to electrical

❑   Nuclear reactors produce radioactive waste, which
     may need to be stored for thousands of years before
     it is safe.

○   The energy output from 1 kg of nuclear fuel is
     millions of times larger than the energy output from
     1 kg of coal.

○   When energy is changed from one form into
     another, the efficiency of the system is given by:

$$\text{efficiency} = \frac{E_{out}}{E_{in}} \times 100\ \%$$

○   The two equations

$$E = Pt \quad \text{and} \quad P = IV$$

can be combined to give:

$$\boxed{E = IVt}$$ where E is energy in J
                                  I is current in A
                                  V is voltage in V
                                  t is time in s

Example

A model pump uses 2 A at 12 V to pump 2500 cm^3 of water 1 m up to a reservoir, in 1.5 minutes.

❑   (a) What is the input energy?
❑   (b) What is the output energy?
○   (c) What is the efficiency of the system?

Step 1   Put the information into symbol form and change to basic units.

I = 2 A
V = 12 V
m = 2500 g = 2.5 kg   (1 cm^3 of water has
                          a mass of 1 g.)
h = 1 m
t = 1.5 mins = 90 s

Step 2   Choose the correct equations.

(a)   energy in   = E_e = IVt

(b)   energy out = E_p = mgh

Step 3   Put the numbers into the equations and calculate the answers.

(a) $E_e = IVt$ = 2 x 12 x 90 = **2160 J**

(b) $E_p = mgh$ = 2.5 x 10 x 1 = **25 J**

(c)

Step 4   Calculate the efficiency.

$$\text{efficiency} = \frac{E_{out}}{E_{in}} \text{ x } 100\,\%$$

$$= \frac{25}{2160} \text{ x } 100\,\% = \mathbf{1.2\,\%}$$

Both the energy in and the energy out can be in any form; the information given in the question indicates which types of energy are relevant.

○ Energy is **degraded** in energy transformations; high grade energy (chemical or electrical) can be easily changed into other forms; low grade energy such as low temperature heat cannot and may be lost to the earth, and then radiated into space; in any energy change, high grade, or useful energy, is always partially changed into low grade, or 'wasted' energy and is therefore degraded.

○ In a **chain reaction**, a neutron hits a nucleus of uranium causing it to split up; this gives two different smaller nuclei and 2 or 3 unattached neutrons, which move on to hit other uranium nuclei and repeat the reaction:

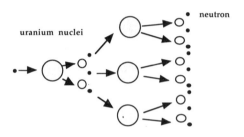

Section 3   Source to consumer

❏   A **voltage is induced** in a conductor:

   (1)   when the conductor is moving in a magnetic
        field,
   (2)   when the magnetic field is changing ,
        eg. using a.c. to produce electromagnetism,
        switching on or off d.c. supply,
        moving the magnet.

❏   In a simple bicycle dynamo a permanent magnet
    rotates (rotor) close to a fixed coil (stator);
    this generates a.c. in the coil.

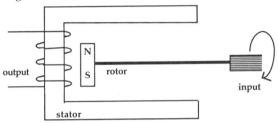

❏   The main parts of a full-size **a.c. generator** are:

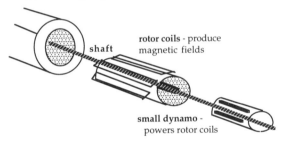

○   In a full-size alternator or generator, the stator coils
    stay still and the rotor coils move; they have a current
    in them and are therefore electromagnets;
    this current is produced by a small dynamo which
    spins on the same shaft as the rotor coils.

○ The main differences between a full-size generator and the simple bicycle dynamo are:

(1) the full-size generator uses an electromagnet as a rotor, rather than a permanent magnet,
(2) the stator of a full-sized generator consists of several coils and carries a large current.

○ The induced voltage can be **increased** by:

(1) increasing the magnetic field strength,
(2) using more turns on the stator coil,
(3) increasing the relative speed of the magnet (rotor) and the stator coil.

❑ The **transformer** consists of two coils of wire, each with a known number of turns, connected by a soft iron core:

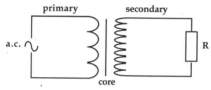

❑ The primary circuit is connected to the a.c. supply and the secondary supplies the resistor or 'load'; there is no electrical connection between the two circuits, only a magnetic one.

❑ Transformers work only on a.c.

❑ A transformer can change the magnitude (size) of an alternating voltage:

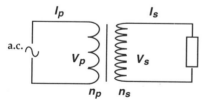

❏   The transformer equation states:

$$\boxed{\dfrac{V_p}{V_s} = \dfrac{n_p}{n_s}}$$

where V_p is the voltage across the primary coil
       V_s is the voltage across the secondary coil
       n_p is the number of turns in the primary coil
       n_s is the number of turns in secondary coil

❏   When $n_s > n_p$, then $V_s > V_p$;
      this is a step-up transformer.

❏   When $n_s < n_p$, then $V_s < V_p$;
      this is a step-down transformer.

❏   *Example*
      How many turns are needed on the secondary coil
      of a mains transformer with 2204 turns on the
      primary coil, if the output voltage is to be 12 V?

Step 1   Put the information into symbol form.

      V_p = 230 V (mains supply)
      V_s = 12 V
      n_p = 2204

Step 2   Choose the correct equation.

      (The transformer equation can be turned upside
      down and is still true; write the equation so that
      the variable to be found is always on the top.)

$$\dfrac{V_s}{V_p} = \dfrac{n_s}{n_p}$$

Step 3   Put the numbers into the equation and
             calculate the answer.

$$\dfrac{V_s}{V_p} = \dfrac{n_s}{n_p} \quad \Rightarrow \quad \dfrac{12}{230} = \dfrac{n_s}{2204}$$

$$n_s = \dfrac{12 \times 2204}{230} = \textbf{115 turns}$$

❑   If the transformer is assumed to be 100% efficient then the power in the primary coil (power in) is equal to the power in the secondary coil (power out):

$$P_p = P_s$$

$$I_p \, V_p = I_s \, V_s$$

This can be written:

$$\frac{V_p}{V_s} = \frac{I_s}{I_p}$$

O   The ratio of voltages and the ratio of number of turns are always equal;
the ratio of voltages, or number of turns, is inversely proportional to the ratio of currents, assuming 100% efficiency.

O   A transformer can approach 100% efficiency; however there will always be some **energy lost:**

(1) heat losses in the coils, reduced by using very low resistance wire
(2) losses due to magnetizing and demagnetizing the core, reduced by using soft iron which does not take much energy to magnetize
(3) losses due to eddy currents and circular currents induced in the core, reduced by laminating, ie. making the core with strips stuck together with insulating glue
(4) sound losses, but usually only in badly designed transformers

O   To find the **efficiency** of a transformer, calculate the power in ($I_p \, V_p$) and the power out ($I_s \, V_s$):

$$\text{efficiency} = \frac{P_{out}}{P_{in}} \; x \; 100 \, \%$$

Example
A transformer has an input voltage of 240 V and input current of 0.1 A. The output from the transformer is 12 V and the current is 1.5 A. Find the efficiency of the transformer.

Step 1   Put the information into symbol form.

$$V_p = 240\text{ V}$$
$$I_p = 0.1\text{ A}$$
$$V_s = 12\text{ V}$$
$$I_s = 1.5\text{ A}$$

Step 2   Choose the correct equations.

$$P_p = V_p I_p$$
$$P_s = V_s I_s$$
$$\text{efficiency} = \frac{P_{out}}{P_{in}} \times 100\ \%$$

Step 3   Put the numbers into the equations and calculate the answers.

$$P_p = V_p I_p = 240 \times 0.1 = 24\text{ W}$$
$$P_s = V_s I_s = 12 \times 1.5 = 18\text{ W}$$
$$\text{efficiency} = \frac{P_{out}}{P_{in}} \times 100\ \%$$
$$= \frac{18}{24} \times 100\ \% = 75\ \%$$

❏   A model **transmission line** consists of:

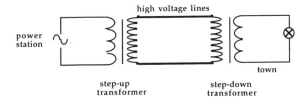

high voltage lines

power station

step-up transformer   step-down transformer   town

❏   High voltages are used in the transmission of electricity to reduce the power loss.

❑ The power loss in the power lines is given by I^2R; this can be reduced by:

(1) making the current as small as possible for a given transmission of power; when the voltage increases, the current decreases; thus high voltage means small current,
(2) using very low resistance wire, eg. copper.

○ *Example*
A model transmission system has two power lines, each with 6 Ω resistance. If the 2 V, 1 A supply is stepped up to 20 V for transmission, what is the power loss in the lines?
(Assume 100% efficiency in the transformers.)

Step 1 Put information into symbol form.
$$R = 6\,\Omega \times 2 = 12\,\Omega\ (\text{since two lines})$$
$$V_p = 2\,V$$
$$V_s = 20\,V$$
$$I_p = 1\,A$$

Step 2 Choose the correct equations.
$$\frac{I_s}{I_p} = \frac{V_p}{V_s} \quad \Rightarrow \quad I_s = \frac{I_p \times V_p}{V_s}$$

$$P = I^2R$$

Step 3 Put the numbers into the equations and calculate the answer.
$$I_s = \frac{I_p \times V_p}{V_s} = \frac{1 \times 2}{20} = 0.1\,A$$

$$P = I^2R = (0.1)^2 \times 12 = \mathbf{0.12\,W}$$

DO NOT FORGET UNITS.

❑ The **National Grid** system transmits electricity around the country; electricity is produced at about 20 kV and immediately stepped up to about 400 kV; at this voltage, overhead lines carry the electricity around the country; regional transformer stations step this down to about 11 kV and feed to local transformers, which reduce it again to 230 V for homes.

Section 4   Heat in the home

❑   **Temperature** is a measure of how hot or cold something is; it is measured in degrees Celsius, **°C.**

❑   **Heat** is a form of energy and is measured in joules, **J.**

❑   If a substance gains heat then its temperature can increase.

There are three methods of **heat transfer:**

❑   (1) **Conduction**
Hot particles vibrate more vigorously than cold; this vibration can be passed from particle to particle and so heat travels through the substance; this is the main method in solids.

❑   (2) **Convection**
A hot gas or liquid is less dense than a cold one, so the hot substance rises and sets up convection currents.

❑   (3) **Radiation**
Energy in the form of electromagnetic rays travels in all directions from a hot body; this is the only method of energy transfer through a vacuum, eg. space.

Reducing heat loss from the home

❑   (1) **Loft insulation** - cuts down heat loss by conduction as the fibre glass used is an insulator; this is important as hot air rises by convection.

❑   (2) **Wall insulation** - cavity walls filled with foam prevents convection currents in cavity.

❑   (3) **Double glazing** - vacuum or thin layer of air between panes of glass prevents convection currents and since air is an insulator cuts heat loss by conduction.

❑   (4) **Floor insulation** - fitted carpets stop heat loss by conduction.

❑   (5) **Foil backed radiators** - foil reflects heat back into the room and helps cut heat loss by radiation.

❑   The heat loss in a given time depends upon the difference in temperature between the inside and the outside of the house. As the dfference increases, the heat loss increases.

❑ For different substances, it takes varying amounts of energy to raise the temperature of 1 kg by 1 °C; the amount of energy required is called the **specific heat capacity** of the substance; it has the symbol c, and is measured in joules per kilogram per degree Celsius, J kg^{-1} °C^{-1}.

❑ When a substance is heated up, without changing state, the heat energy required is:

$$E_h = c\, m\, \Delta T$$

where E_h is the heat in J

c is the specific heat capacity in J kg^{-1} °C^{-1}

m is the mass in kg

ΔT is the **change** in temperature in °C

❑ *Example*
What is the final temperature when 150 kJ of energy is given to 2 kg of water at 20 °C?

Step 1 Put information into symbol form and change to basic units.

$E_h = 150$ kJ $= 150\ 000$ J

$m = 2$ kg

$c_{\text{water}} = 4180$ J kg^{-1} °C^{-1} (from data tables)

$T_{\text{initial}} = 20$ °C

Step 2 Choose the correct equation,

$$E_h = c\, m\, \Delta T \quad \Rightarrow \quad \Delta T = \frac{E_h}{c\, m}$$

Step 3 Put the numbers into the equation and calculate the answer.

$$\Delta T = \frac{E_h}{c\, m} = \frac{150\ 000}{4180 \times 2} = 17.9\ °C$$

Final temperature $= T_{\text{initial}} + \Delta T = 20 + 17.9 = \mathbf{37.9\ °C}$

○ Heat can be produced from many other forms of energy, eg. electrical, kinetic, potential; since energy is conserved, the amount of heat energy can be found by calculating the other form.

○ Useful equations are:

$$E = P\,t \qquad E_e = I\,V\,t \qquad E_k = \frac{1}{2}m\,v^2$$
$$E_p = m\,g\,h \qquad\qquad E_w = F\,d$$

Any of these can then be put equal to $c\,m\,\Delta T$ provided no energy is 'lost', ie. the system is 100 % efficient.

Example
If a 2 kW immersion heater takes 20 minutes to raise the temperature of 20 kg of water by 24 °C, find the heat which is lost.

Step 1 Put the information into symbol form and change to basic units.

P = 2000 W
t = 20 min = 1200 s
m = 20 kg
Δt = 25 °C
C_{water} = 4180 J kg^{-1} °C^{-1} (from data tables)

Step 2 Choose the correct equations.

E = $P\,t$
E_h = $c\,m\,\Delta T$

Step 3 Put the numbers into the equations and calculate the answer.

E = $P\,t$ = 2000 x 1200 = 2 400 000 J
E_h = $c\,m\,\Delta t$ = 4180 x 20 x 24 = 2 006 400 J

Energy lost = 2 400 000 - 2 006 400
= **394 000 J**

❑ The three states of matter are solid, liquid and gas.

❑ The **changes of state** are :

Evaporation	-	liquid to gas
Condensation	-	gas to liquid
Freezing	-	liquid to solid
Melting	-	solid to liquid

❑   **Melting**   **Evaporation**

Solid	⇌	Liquid	⇌	Gas

          Freezing   **Condensation**

For either change ──▶ energy must be provided;

for either change ◀── energy is given out.

❑ When a substance changes state, its temperature remains the same until the change of state is complete.

❑ The amount of energy needed to change state depends only on the mass of the substance and what it is.

❑ To change 1 kg of a substance from solid to liquid (or liquid to solid) involves energy equal to the **specific latent heat of fusion, L_{fusion}** ; this is different for each substance.

❑ To change 1 kg of a substance from liquid to gas (or gas to liquid) involves energy equal to the **specific latent heat of vaporisation, $L_{vaporisation}$** ; this is different for each substance.

○ The specific latent heat of vaporisation is always larger than the specific latent heat of fusion; it takes more energy for molecules to break right away from the rest and form a gas, than it does to break the bonds holding molecules, in order to form a liquid.

Applications involving changes of state

❑ (1) **Cool boxes**
The sides are well insulated to stop heat getting in;
a plastic pack of chemicals is frozen in a freezer,
then placed on top of the food, as hot air rises;
the pack absorbs the heat and melts, thus
keeping the food cool.

❑ (2) **Refrigerators**
A fluid, freon, with a very small latent heat of
vaporisation and a low boiling point, is used;
the freon is easily changed into a gas;
the liquid freon flows through a small valve
and evaporates, using heat absorbed from the
food inside the refrigerator;
the gas passes into a compressor pump and
turns back into a liquid, at the back of the fridge;
this gives out the heat into the room.

○ When a substance changes state, the heat energy
required is:

$$E_h = m\,L$$

where E_h is the heat in J
  m is the mass in kg
  L is the specific latent heat in J kg^{-1}

○ The above equation is true for all changes of state as
long as the correct latent heat is used.

○   *Example*
How much energy is required to change 3 kg of
water at 20 °C all into steam at 100 °C?

Step 1   Put information into symbol form.

m = 3 kg
$T_{initial}$ = 20 °C
T_{final} = 100 °C,   therefore ΔT = 80 °C
c_{water} = 4180 J k^{-1} °C^{-1}
$L_{vaporisation\ for\ water}$ = 2.26 x 10^6 J kg^{-1}

Step 2   Choose the correct equations.

$E_h = c\,m\,\Delta T$
$E_h = m\,L$

Step 3   Put the numbers into the equations and
calculate the answers.

(1) to raise to boiling

$E_h = c\,m\,\Delta T$ = 4180x 3 x 80 = 1 003 200 J

(2) to turn into gas

$E_h = m\,L$ = 3 x 2.26 x 10^6 = 6 780 000 J

Total energy = 1 003 200 + 6 780 000 = **7 783 000 J**

DO NOT FORGET UNITS.

This type of question must be done in two parts:
(i)   Calculate the energy needed to bring water to boiling.
(ii) Calculate the energy to turn the water into steam.

UNIT 7   SPACE PHYSICS

Section 1   Signals from space

❑   The **universe** consists of many galaxies separated by empty space.

❑   Each **galaxy**, eg. the Milky Way, has many solar systems (like our own) and stars without planets.

❑   Each **solar system** has a central star, eg. the Sun.

❑   A **planet** orbits a star, eg. the Earth orbits the Sun.

❑   Some of the planets have their own **moons** orbiting them.

○   A **light year** is the distance, **d**, which light travels in one year; it is used as a unit of distance in astronomy.

○   A light year can be calculated using the equation:

$$d = v\,t$$

where v is the speed of light in m s^{-1}
        t is one year in seconds

1 light year $= 3 \times 10^8 \times 365 \times 24 \times 60 \times 60$ m
             $= 9.46 \times 10^{15}$ m

❑   To reach Earth, light takes:

(1) about 8 minutes from the Sun,
(2) about 4.3 years from the next nearest star,
(3) about 100 000 years from the other side of our galaxy.

A refracting telescope

❑

objective lens | light tight tubes | eyepiece lens

❑   The objective lens produces an image which is magnified by the eyepiece.

○   The image is brighter if the objective lens has a larger diameter; the larger the objective lens is, the more light is allowed into the telescope.

○ For a convex lens, the position of any image can be found by drawing two rays from the top of the object:

  (1) a ray through the centre of the lens which does not change direction,
  (2) a ray parallel to the principal axis, until it reaches the lens, which then passes through the focus.

○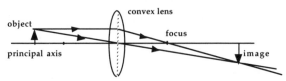

○ A magnifying glass is a convex lens with the object placed between the lens and the focus.

○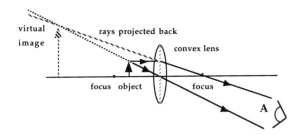

○ In this case the construction rays do not meet, but when projected back they do meet;
since light does not actually pass through this point the image is **virtual**;
however a human eye placed at **A** will bring the light to a focus and the virtual magnified image is seen;
it is erect, ie. the same way up as the object.

❑ Different colours of light have different wavelengths.

❑ The wavelength of red light is longer than that of green light which is longer than that of blue light:

$$\lambda_r > \lambda_g > \lambda_b$$

❑ White light is made up of all the colours of the rainbow; a prism will split white light into its component colours:

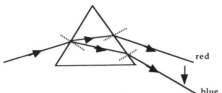

❑ The visible spectrum (rainbow colours) is given by (**ROYGBIV**):

Red Orange Yellow Green Blue Indigo Violet

❑ Every element produces a line spectrum which is unique to that element; thus by studying the line spectra given by any source, the atoms within that source can be identified.

❑ There are a number of waves which travel at the speed of light; they differ in their wavelength and frequency.

○ These waves are members of the **electromagnetic spectrum**:

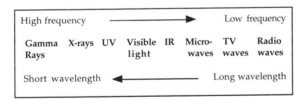

❑ Telescopes, called 'radio telescopes', have been designed to detect radio waves.

○ Energy is emitted from objects in space at many different wavelengths (or frequencies); in order to get a full picture of the universe information has to be collected at all wavelengths; different kinds of telescope are used to detect each range of wavelengths; thus many types of telescope are needed.

Detectors for members of the electromagnetic spectrum are:

○ Gamma rays   Geiger- Muller tube and scaler

○ X-rays   Photographic plates

○ Ultra violet   Fluorescent paint (absorbs energy in the ultra violet and re-emits in the visible part of the spectrum)

○ Visible light   Human eye or photographic film

○ Infra red (heat radiation)   Blackened thermometer (so that it absorbs radiation better) or phototransistor and meter

○ Microwaves   Diode probe and meter

○ TV waves   Aerial and television set

○ Radio waves   Aerial and radio set

Section 2   Space travel

❏   A rocket is pushed forward because the 'propellant' is pushed back.

❏   A pushes **B** and **B** pushes **A** back,
     eg. bat pushes ball and ball pushes back on bat.

○   **Newton's Third Law** states that
     " If **A** exerts a force on **B**, **B** exerts an equal and opposite force on **A**".

○   **A** and **B** are known as "Newton pairs",
     eg.

A is the force of propellant gases
   on the rocket;
B is the force of the rocket on
   propellant gases.

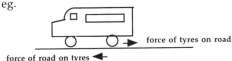

○   In each case the nouns change position,
     eg.

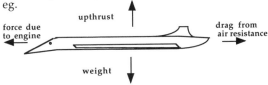

○   "Newton pairs" always act on different objects,
     e.g. on the road and on the tyres.

○   There may be many "Newton pairs" acting,
     eg.

Weight
force of Earth on plane = force of plane on Earth

Upthrust
force of displaced air on plane = force of plane on displaced air

Drag
frictional force of air on plane = force of plane on air

Engine
force of plane on expelled gases = force of gases on plane

○ Do not confuse **balanced** forces which act on the **same object** with **"Newton pairs"** which always act on **different objects**, e.g. if the aircraft is in level flight at a constant speed then the upthrust is balanced by the weight (both acting on the plane) and the force due to the engine is balanced by the drag from the air resistance (both acting on the plane).

❑ The **thrust** from an engine provides the force to make the object accelerate.

❑ *Example*
What is the acceleration of the 1200 kg truck shown below?

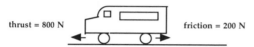

thrust = 800 N   friction = 200 N

Step 1   Put information into symbol form.

m = 1200 kg
Thrust = 800 N F = Thrust - Friction
Friction = 200 N   = 800 - 200 = 600 N

Step 2   Choose the correct equation.

$$F = m\,a \quad => \quad a = \frac{F}{m}$$

Step 3   Put the numbers into the equation and calculate the answer.

$$a = \frac{F}{m} = \frac{600}{1200} = 0.5 \text{ m s}^{-2}$$

DO NOT FORGET UNITS.

Always make sure the resultant force is calculated before using Newton's Second Law.

❑ *Example 2*
What is the acceleration upwards of the 500 kg
rocket, if the thrust is 25 000 N?

Step 1   Draw a diagram showing all the forces.

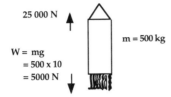

25 000 N

W = mg
  = 500 x 10
  = 5000 N

m = 500 kg

(Since the object is moving vertically, the force due to
gravity (weight) must be taken into account although
it is not mentioned in the question.)

Step 2   Put information into symbol form.

m = 500 kg
Thrust = 25 000 N F = Thrust - Weight
Weight = 5000 N   = 25 000 - 5000
                            = 20 000 N

Step 3   Choose the correct equation.

$$F = m\,a \quad => \quad a = \frac{F}{m}$$

Step 4   Put the numbers into the equation and
calculate the answer.

$$a = \frac{F}{m} = \frac{20\,000}{500} = 40 \text{ m s}^{-2}$$

DO NOT FORGET UNITS.

❑   When a rocket in space has reached the desired
speed, the engines can be switched off;
space is a vacuum, so there are no frictional forces
acting on the rocket once the engine is off;
provided there is no gravitational pull from planets,
there are no forces;
therefore the rocket continues in the same direction
at the same speed;
this is an example of Newton's First Law.

❑   The **force of gravity**, weight, near the Earth's surface,
gives all objects the same acceleration (10 m s^{-2});
this is always true as long as air resistance can be
ignored.

❑   The weight of an object on the Moon or other planets is different from its weight on Earth.

○   Acceleration due to gravity, g, is 10 m s^{-2} on Earth; the gravitational field strength is 10 N kg^{-1} on Earth; both have the same numerical value but the units are different; this is true for all planets.

○   The acceleration due to gravity and the gravitational field strength can be shown to be equivalent:

The gravitational field strength, g, is the weight per unit mass:

$$g = \frac{W}{m}$$

From the definition of weight and Newton's Second law, the weight of a freely falling body is given by:

$$w = ma_g \qquad \text{where } a_g \text{ is the}$$
acceleration due to gravity

Combining these two expressions:

$$g = \frac{W}{m} = \frac{ma_g}{m} = a_g$$

The usual symbol is ' g '.

The units of both, ms^{-2} and N kg^{-1}, are also equivalent.

○   If the gravitational field strength for any planet is given then the acceleration is known.

○ *Example*
   If the gravitational field strength on Jupiter is
   26 N kg^{-1}, what is the weight of an 80 kg man?

   Step 1 Put information into symbol form.

   m = 80 kg
   g = 26 N kg^{-1}

   Step 2 Choose the correct equation.

   $W = mg$

   Step 3 Put the numbers into the equation and
   calculate the answer.

   $W = mg$ = 80 x 26 = **2080 N**

   DO NOT FORGET UNITS.

❏ In space, far away from any planets or stars, there is
   practically no force due to gravity;
   an object is said to be **weightless.**

❏ An object in **free fall** appears to be weightless;
   this is what happens to astronauts in a spacecraft;
   both the spacecraft and the astronauts are falling
   towards Earth at the same rate.

○ **Inertia** is the property of an object which makes it
   hard to get the object moving;
   inertia also makes it hard to stop the object once it is
   moving;
   inertia varies with mass.

○ The weight of a body decreases as it gets further
   away from Earth, ie. the distance from Earth
   increases.

❏ **Friction** causes energy to be lost in the form of heat,
   eg. when a spacecraft re-enters the Earth's
   atmosphere from space, the kinetic energy of the
   spacecraft is changed into heat.

○ The principle of conservation of energy can be used to find the temperature rise.

$$E_k = E_h$$
$$\frac{1}{2} m v^2 = c\, m\, \Delta T$$

$$E_w = E_h$$
$$F d = c\, m\, \Delta T$$

○ The spacecraft is painted black to radiate maximum energy and protected by a silica coating, which melts at a very high temperature and is a very poor conductor.

❑ A projectile projected horizontally will follow a curved path as shown:

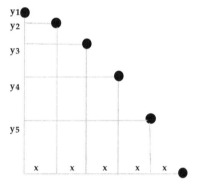

❑ **Horizontally** the distance, **x,** travelled in a fixed time, is always constant;
therefore **the horizontal speed is constant**;
this is true because there are no forces acting horizontally (provided air resistance is negligible).

❑ **Vertically**, the distance, **y**, travelled in a fixed time, increases;
gravity is acting on the object;
therefore the vertical speed increases;
the vertical acceleration is constant (10 m s^{-2}).

○ Horizontal and vertical motion are **independent**; only time is common.

○ A satellite orbiting the Earth is continually falling to Earth, just like any other projectile; as the satellite is moving so fast, the Earth curves away from it as fast as it falls; thus the satellite never reaches Earth but continues in orbit.

○ *Example*
An aircraft travelling horizontally at 200 m s^{-1} drops a package which hits the ground 6 s later.

Ignoring air resistance find:
(a) how fast package is going vertically just before it lands
(b) how fast it is going horizontally just before it lands,
(c) the height of the aircraft,
(d) how far the package travels horizontally (range),
(e) where the plane is, compared to the package, when the package lands.

Step 1 Divide the page into two halves and put the information into symbol form.

Vertical

t = 6 s

u_v = 0 (as it leaves plane)

a_v = 10 m s^{-2} (gravity)

Horizontal

t = 6 s

u_h = 200 m s^{-1} (same as plane)

a_h = 0

(u_v, a_v and a_h are not given but are determined from properties of projectiles.)

Step 2 Choose the correct equations.

(a) $v = u + a t$

(b) $u_h = v_h$
(horizontal speed constant)

Step 3 Put the numbers into the equations and calculate the answers.

(a) $v = u + a t$

v_v = 0 + 10 × 6

  = 60 m s^{-1}

(b) $u_h = v_h = 200$ m s^{-1}

Step 4   To find the distances sketch speed - time
graphs;
the distances are the areas under the graphs.

(c)   vertical velocity
in m s⁻¹

(d)   horizontal velocity
in m s⁻¹

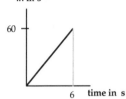

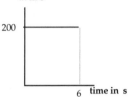

$d_v = \frac{1}{2}(60 \times 6) = $ **180 m**

$d_h = 200 \times 6$

$= $ **1200 m**

(e)   The package is travelling horizontally at the
same speed as the plane;
thus if the plane does not change direction or speed,
after 6 s it will be 180 m vertically above the package.

PRACTICAL ABILITIES

You are assessed by your own teacher on:

(a) **Practical techniques**   -   16 marks
(b) **Two practical investigations**   -   48 marks

The grade which you are allocated will depend on the marks that you achieve, subject to external moderation:

> Grade **1** - 64 - 55 marks
> Grade **2** - 54 - 46 marks
> Grade **3** - 45 - 39 marks
> Grade **4** - 38 - 30 marks
> Grade **5** - 29 - 19 marks
> Grade **7** - less than 19 marks

PRACTICAL TECHNIQUES

You should be given the opportunity to practise the techniques before you are assessed on them.
You gain 2 marks for each technique you successfully complete.
There are eight techniques in all.

❑   **1. Measure the speed of a moving object**
You will use a light gate to measure the time for a card to pass.
Calculate the speed using: length of card.
                                                time
You must agrree closely with your teacher's result.

❑   **2. Measure the focal length of a convex lens**
You will be given five different lenses and must pick out the one with the particular focal length your teacher asks for.

❑   **3. Measure angles of incidence and reflection**
You will be given a glass block and a piece of paper with the direction of the incident ray and the position of the glass block on it.
You must draw the normal and the direction of the refracted ray and measure the angles of incidence and reflection.

title??

in bold

❑   **4. Detect open and short circuits**
You will be given three different boards and must find where the fault is and which type for each board.

❏   5. **Measure the current and voltage for a component**
      You must connect the ammeter (in series) and
      the voltmeter (in parallel) and take readings
      accurately.
❏   6. **Connect an oscilloscope to an a.c. supply and
      read the peak voltage**
      You must make the connections and adjust
      both the time-base and the Y-gain controls to
      obtain a clear pattern;
      use the Y-gain scale to work out the voltage.

❏   7. **Set up a voltage divider and then adjust to give
      1 volt**
      You must be able to do this without a circuit
      diagram.

❏   8. **Wire up a circuit with both series and parallel
      parts, given the circuit diagram**
      You must make sure that all the components
      are in the right order and that the ammeter
      reading is positive.

PRACTICAL INVESTIGATIONS

You will be given a problem to discuss in a small group. After the initial discussion you must take responsibility for your own investigation and work independently.
You will be marked on 13 different aspects of your investigation.

☐   1.   Pick out one part of the problem to investigate; after the discussion you must choose one factor that is likely to affect the answer and can be measured (**1 mark**).

☐   2.   Make a clear statement of the aim of your investigation (**1 mark**).

☐   3.   State a working hypothesis;
this means state exactly what you expect the result of your investigation to be;
you **must** say whether you expect what is being measured to increase or decrease (vary is not good enough) or remain the same;
it does not matter if you are wrong since you will have a chance to change your mind later (**1 mark**).

☐   4.   Decide exactly what to measure and how you are going to do it in the lab (**2 marks**).

☐   5.   You carry out the experiment properly and safely (**1 mark**).

☐   6.   You identify the variable which you are going to be able to choose values for (called the independent variable) (**1 mark**) and allow it to change over a suitable range, as wide as possible (**1 mark**).

☐   7.   All other relevant variables are kept constant; apart from the two being measured everything else must be kept the same to make the experiment fair (**1 mark**);
make a written statement of the things you are keeping constant (**1 mark**).

❑   **8.**   Make valid measurements of the two dependent variables **(1 mark)**; take repeated measurements and an average **OR** give a reason for not taking an average, **in writing (1 mark)**.

❑   **9.**   Produce a table of results with suitable headings **(1 mark)** and units **(1 mark)**.

❑   **10.**   Present your results in a chart or a graph of a suitable size and scale **(1 mark)**; both axes are labelled with variable and units **(1 mark)**; all points on the graph are marked clearly (use **+**) and accurately **(1 mark)**; a straight line or smooth curve is drawn through the points **OR** a statement is made that there is no such curve possible **OR** draw a bar chart **(1 mark)**.

❑   **11.**   Draw a valid conclusion from your results **OR** state that no firm conclusion can be drawn **(1 mark)**.

❑   **12.**   Use the results to adapt your hypothesis if necessary; you must state, **in writing**, whether your original idea was correct, or needs changing or your results do not allow you to decide **(1 mark)**.

❑   **13.**   Write up your experiment; you must include enough detail so that anyone else reading it could carry out the experiment; include a labelled diagram of the apparatus **(1 mark)** and the method used to measure each of the variables **(2 marks)**; also include a description of how the variable you set (the independent variable) was changed **(1 mark)**.

You will have to complete at least 2 investigations. Each investigation has a maximum mark of 24.

The **total mark** achieved on the investigations will be added to your mark on techniques to obtain your overall grade.

QUANTITIES AND UNITS

	Quantity	Symbol	Unit (basic unit first)
❑	length	l	m, mm, cm , km
❑	area	A	m^2, cm^2, mm^2
❑	volume	V	m^3, cm^3, mm^3
❑	distance	d	m, cm, km
❑	mass	m	kg, g
❑	weight	W	N
❑	time	t	s, min, hr
❑	half life	τ	s, min, hr
❑	speed	v	$m\ s^{-1}$, m.p.h.
❑	acceleration	a	$m\ s^{-2}$
❑	acc. due to gravity	g	$10\ m\ s^{-2}$
❑	frequency	f	Hz, kHz
❑	wavelength	λ	m, cm
❑	period	T	s
❑	energy	E	J
❑	work	E_W	J
❑	force	F	N
❑	power	P	W
◯	power of lens	P	D
❑	current	I	A
❑	voltage (p.d..)	V	V
❑	resistance	R	Ω
◯	charge	Q	C
❑	temperature	T	^oC
❑	specific heat capacity	c	$J\ kg^{-1}\ ^oC^{-1}$
◯	specific latent heat	L	$J\ kg^{-1}$
◯	absorbed dose	D	Gy
❑	dose equivalent	H	Sv
◯	gravitational field strength	g	$N\ kg^{-1}$

FORMULAE

- $v = f \, \lambda$

- $f = \dfrac{1}{T}$ or $T = \dfrac{1}{f}$

- $d = v \, t$ (for constant speed)

- $F = m \, a$ (Newton's Second Law)

- $W = m \, g$

- $a = \dfrac{v - u}{t}$

- $v = u + a \, t$

- $E_W = F \, d$

- $E_p = m \, g \, h$

- $E_k = \dfrac{1}{2} m \, v^2$

- $v = \sqrt{2 \, g \, h}$ since $E_k = E_p$
(Do not use if energy is 'lost' due to friction.)

- $E = P \, t$ or $P = \dfrac{E}{t}$

- Distance = area under speed - time graph

- $\overline{v}$ = average speed = $\dfrac{\text{total distance travelled}}{\text{total time taken}}$

- $E_h = c \, m \, \Delta T$

- $E_h = m \, L$

- $L_{vaporisation}$ - if boiling or condensing

- L_{fusion} - if melting or freezing

- $Q = I \, t$

- $V = I \, R$

- $P = I \, V = I^2 R = \dfrac{V^2}{R}$

- $E = I \, V \, t = I^2 R \times t = \dfrac{V^2}{R} \times t$

○ $R_T = R_1 + R_2 + R_3 + ...$ resistors in series

○ $\dfrac{1}{R_T} = \dfrac{1}{R_1} + \dfrac{1}{R_2} + \dfrac{1}{R_3} + ...$ resistors in parallel

❑
○ $\dfrac{V_s}{V_p} = \dfrac{N_s}{N_p} = \dfrac{I_p}{I_s}$ Transformer equation
s indicates secondary,
p indicates primary circuit.

❑   efficiency $= \dfrac{E_{out}}{E_{in}} \times 100\%$ or $\dfrac{P_{out}}{P_{in}} \times 100\%$

○   power of lens $= \dfrac{1}{\text{focal length (in metres)}}$

❑   voltage gain $= \dfrac{\text{voltage out}}{\text{voltage in}}$

❑   power gain $= \dfrac{\text{power out}}{\text{power in}}$

DRAWING AND INTERPRETING GRAPHS

Drawing graphs

❑   1. If you have to choose the scale of the axes:
(a) find the maximum value needed for each axis,
(b) make the scales simple to interpret (avoid using 1 box to represent 3 units),
(c) **x-axis:** the numbers usually rise in regular intervals (the independent variable),
(d) **y-axis:** the experimental results, usually irregular.

❑   2. Label the axes clearly with both the name of the variable and the units.

❑   3. When marking the points use a **+.** Double check any points that are well away from the others.

❑   4. Join the points with a smooth line. If the graph is obviously a straight line then use a ruler to draw the best fitting line that you can.

Interpreting graphs

❑   1. (a) Check very carefully the information given in the question.
(b) Check the variables plotted on the axes.
(c) Check the units of the variables.

❑   2. Read values carefully.

❑   3. To find value of **x** given that of **y,**
(a) draw a line across from the given value of **y,** parallel to the **x**-axis, until it meets the curve,
(b) draw a line down from that point to the **x**-axis, parallel to the **y**-axis and read the value on the **x**-axis.

USING EQUATIONS

There are no short cuts!

❏ 1. **Learn the formulae.** You must know all of them, **accurately.**

❏ 2. Read the question carefully and even if you do not know how to do it, follow the steps below. If you know your formulae you may see the way to handle the question once you have started.

❏ 3. Write out the values given in the question using symbol, value and units, including the symbol for the required answer:

symbol = value and units

eg. v = 200 cm s^{-1}

❏ 4. Change any non-standard units to the basic unit (shown first in the list of units),

eg. v = 0.2 m s^{-1}

❏ 5. Write down the equation which involves the symbols that you have, in its usual form,

eg. $E_h = c \, m \, \Delta T$

❏ 6. Rearrange the equation so that the quantity you are trying to find is on its own on the left hand side of the equation,

eg. $\Delta T = \dfrac{E_h}{c \, m}$

❏ 7. Fill in the figures you have, and **write** them down.
(You only get marks for what is on paper!)

❏ 8. Do the calculation and write down the answer.

❏ 9. Check that you have included units in your answer and have not written too many figures (see significant figures).

SIGNIFICANT FIGURES

❏   An answer of 3 and 3.0 may appear the same but
they mean different things.
3 means the answer is above 2.5 and below 3.5
(the answer is to 1 significant figure).
3.0 means the answer is above 2.95 and below 3.05
(the answer is to 2 significant figures).

❏   Writing down all the numbers the calculator gives
you, eg. 3.0467812, is **wrong** because it claims you
know the answer far more accurately than any
information you have been given.

❏   In general give answers to **three significant figures**
at most.
Round up the next figure.
If the fourth figure is a 5 or above, add one to the
third figure.
If the fourth figure is below 5, leave the third figure
alone, eg. 3.0467812 becomes 3.05.

❏   If using a graph to find information, only use two
significant figures.

SCIENTIFIC NOTATION

☐ Many numbers in physics are expressed in scientific notation,

eg. 3×10^8 m s^{-1} is the speed of light.

☐ When written out in full:

1×10^9 = 1 000 000 000
3×10^8 = 300 000 000
5.79×10^7 = 57 900 000

In each case the number of figures, after the first, is given by the value of the indices.

☐ When the indices have a negative value, then the number is less than one.

☐ When written out in full:

1×10^{-3} = 0.001
3×10^{-4} = 0.0003
5.79×10^{-5} = 0.0000579

In each case, the value of the index gives the number of zeroes, with the decimal point placed after the first zero.

☐ When putting into calculator:

5×10^9 = | 5 | | EXP | | 9 |

7×10^{-6} = | 7 | | EXP | | 6 | | -/+ |

Do not put in the 10 as well.

☐ **Prefixes** are used with the basic units instead of using scientific notation:

Tera (T)	=	10^{12}	milli (m)	=	10^{-3}
Giga (G)	=	10^9	micro (μ)	=	10^{-6}
Mega (M)	=	10^6	nano (n)	=	10^{-9}
Kilo (k)	=	10^3	pico (p)	=	10^{-12}

☐ All units must be changed to the basic, if given with a prefix.

☐ The only exception is **mass** where the basic unit is the **kg**.

PROPORTIONALITY

❑ Many quantities in physics are **directly proportional** to each other. A certain change in one will always result in exactly the same change in the other.

❑

❑ 1. **Graph A**
As **x** varies, so does **y** and the graph formula is **y = mx**, where **m** is the slope or gradient:

$$m = \frac{y_2 - y_1}{x_2 - x_1}$$

❑ 2. **Graph B.**
As **x** varies, so does **y** but when **x = 0**, **y** has a value. The graph formula is **y = mx +c.**
m is still the gradient found as above.
c is the value of **y** when **x = 0**.

❑ 3. **Graph C.**
As **x** increases, **y** decreases.
Since the graph is a curve, it is not easy to see how **x** and **y** are related.
To check, work out **1/x** for each point and replot the points with **y** against **1/x**.
If this gives a straight line through the origin, as shown in **graph D**, then **y** is said to be **indirectly proportional** to x.
The graph formula is $y = \dfrac{m}{x}$.

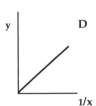